ARCHITECTURAL SKETCHING AND RENDERING
TECHNIQUES FOR DESIGNERS AND ARTISTS

ARCHITECTURAL SKETCHING AND RENDERING

TECHNIQUES FOR DESIGNERS AND ARTISTS

EDITED BY STEPHEN KLIMENT
FOREWORD BY CESAR PELLI

WHITNEY LIBRARY OF DESIGN
an imprint of Watson-Guptill Publications/New York

Copyright © 1984 by Whitney Library of Design

**First published 1984 in New York by the Whitney Library of Design,
an imprint of Watson-Guptill Publications,
a division of VNU Business Media, Inc.,
770 Broadway, New York, NY 10003
www.wgpub.com**

Library of Congress Cataloging in Publication Data
Kliment, Stephen A.
  Architectural sketching and rendering.
  Bibliography: p.
  Includes index.
  1. Architectural drawing—Technique.   2. Architectural
rendering—Technique.   I. Title.
NA2708.K59   1984   720'.28'4   84-2404
ISBN 0-8230-7052-2 (cloth)
ISBN 0-8230-7053-0 (soft)

Distributed in the United Kingdom by Phaidon Press Ltd., Littlegate
House, St. Ebbe's St., Oxford

Manufactured in U.S.A.

First Printing, 1984

17 18 19 20/09 08 07 06

ACKNOWLEDGMENTS

This book would still be a mix of fine but unconnected parts had it not been for the steady and persevering hand of Susan Davis, development editor at Whitney Library of Design, who painstakingly reviewed every line of the original texts and spliced it all together into a seamless whole.

Jay Anning's design brings out the practical nature of the contents, imposing unity over widely different pieces of text and artwork and making these into a book that is both handsome and usable. His jacket strongly evokes the book's theme. I thank Areta Buk for carrying the design concept through to its details.

Carole Forman diligently pursued permissions and calmly completed the other support tasks demanded by this book. I also thank Ellen Greene for dealing with a complex production job.

Donald Holden, David Lewis, and Virginia Croft offered valuable counsel.

Last, but not least, thanks are due to Gerald Allen and Richard Oliver, Harry Borgman, Norman Diekman and John Pile, David Gebhard and Deborah Nevins, Jean Ferriss Leich, the late Arthur Guptill, Susan Meyer, Paul Hogarth, Ferdinand Petrie, Peter Probyn, and Richard Downer. They created the original strands from which this cloth was woven.

Stephen A. Kliment
Executive Editor
Whitney Library of Design

CONTENTS

FOREWORD

Architectural drawings are means to an end. That end is the building. They are of a different nature than drawings of architecture done by artists. For an artist, it is the architecture that is the means to a pictorial end. There is a more profound difference in that an architectural drawing is concerned with architectural issues, those that are important to the architectural culture of its time; an art drawing is concerned with artistic issues, those that are important to the pictorial art culture. At least in our times, the issues these two cultures are concerned with are substantially different from each other, although the gap is narrowing. Even if an architect draws very well and is influenced by the art of his or her times and is now selling drawings in the art market, the value of the work will depend on the worth of the architectural thoughts the drawings convey.

When I look at an architectural drawing, I react first to its beauty, its quality as pure drawing. This predisposes me to my next impression, but it is not enough in itself; I expect the drawings to engage me with an architectural issue. The most immediate is: Is the architecture depicted beautiful? Is it good architecture? Am I in any way moved by the forms or intrigued by the ideas?

A beautiful drawing may describe an ugly or bad building. That drawing will be of no interest to me. It is a poor architectural drawing, no matter how skillfully it may have been rendered. A crude drawing conveying a powerful architectural idea becomes beautiful. If the draftsman is a good architect, the drawing may be crude but it will never be ugly. The eye is more important than the hand. And the mind should rule them both.

An architectural drawing is primarily an element for communication; a good drawing will support and strengthen the intention of the architecture: A drawing describing the beauty of a building needs to be beautiful itself. A drawing describing the strength of a form needs to be itself strong and a drawing describing the clarity of a plan needs to be itself clear and intelligent.

A good architectural drawing is a strongly biased presentation of an architecture. Drawings derive most of their fascination from this condition. The qualities the architect/draftsman is interested in are heightened; the possible weaknesses are ignored or suppressed. We are in immediate touch with the essence of an architectural possibility and this can be exhilarating. We are also aware that the process is a form of deception in that we see only a partial, selected, and sometimes distorted view of reality. Even when we question the reality the drawings present to us, we can be fascinated by the suggested architecture or by the ideas they convey. The drawn architecture of Etienne-Louis Boullée, Antonio Sant'Elia, and Hugh Ferriss has a reality in our minds that is more significant and more influential than that of most buildings.

Architecture usually starts with a mark of a pencil on paper. That mark is not just a record of a thought but it starts at that moment to affect the development of forms and ideas of the building to be. We had better be in control of the process or those lines on paper may decide it for us. Moreover, we need to be aware of the design process and the role that drawing plays in it. Finally, we need to master the necessary skills and learn to recognize the opportunities that drawing offers us.

Cesar Pelli

PART ONE
MAKING A START

The chapters in the first part of this book will give you a solid grounding in the use of two of the most versatile media available to the artist and designer: pencil and ink.

You can use the pencil to obtain a wide range of effects. But how well you do later is determined largely at a very early stage by seriously attending to detail, even to such seemingly trivial steps as the way you sharpen your pencil and the way you hold it. Begin by practicing lines; if you have already mastered this step, move on to drawing tones, as shown in Chapter 4. Tones are what give character to your sketches, and the two basic types of tone (flat and graded) that you will find demonstrated in the chapter should be only a starting point for you to develop your own preferred style.

The other great sketching medium is ink. Whether you apply it by pen or by brush, it is one of the most subtle media known, with techniques yielding a vast range of effects to serve you in shaping the mood of your drawing. The methods range from lines to tones. You can use lines in an infinite combination of straight and curved, thick and fine, continuous, broken or overlapping, or even in varying weights. With lines as a starter, you can use your pen or brush to build up a range of textures and tones and obtain almost microscopic control over the surfaces and details of a building and its parts.

By way of emphasis, a special chapter suggests methods of creating tonal values once you have mastered line. To brush up on your grasp of perspective, another chapter in this section provides a simple but effective way of breaking a building down into its component shapes and of relating what you see to what you show on paper.

At this point you should have the tools needed to capture architecture itself—modern or traditional—whether *you* designed the work or whether you wish to sketch the work of others.

CHAPTER ONE
YOUR STUDIO

Even before you pick up a pencil or pen take the time to set up your studio so that you can work efficiently from the beginning. The most important elements to consider are drawing surfaces and lighting.

Drawing Board. Although you can use an ordinary table or even a desk to work on, a portable wooden drawing board is preferable. These boards are quite handy and come in a variety of sizes, ranging from 16″ × 20″ (41 × 51 cm) to 31″ × 42″ (79 × 107 cm). You can tape your paper to the board with masking tape and be ready to work. These boards are also ideal for sketching outdoors or in a drawing class.

Drawing Table. Many artists or designers prefer working at a regular artist's drawing board or a drafting table. A drawing board can be tilted and locked at any comfortable working angle, while some can even be lowered or raised up to 40″ (102 cm). They can be tilted to a horizontal position for use as cutting tables. Many tables of this type can be folded for easy storage, which is helpful if you have a space problem. There are also more expensive types of drawing boards, which have been perfectly counterbalanced and can be tilted and raised simultaneously—an excellent feature.

It is obvious that there are many types of drawing tables available in every price range. You will have to be the judge of which type suits your needs best.

Taboret and Chair. The taboret is a type of table that is handy for storing tools, and it can double as a convenient table on which to set things while you are working. Again, many types are available at various prices. Of course you may prefer using a wooden board or an old table rather than buying another piece of furniture.

As for seating, any comfortable chair will do, but many artists prefer a chair with armrests that swivels and has casters for ease of movement.

Lighting. If you are going to be working by artificial light, you should invest in a fluorescent lamp. This is an excellent type of light for artists because it provides a very bright, uniform light that casts soft shadows. Some fluorescent lamps are designed so that they can be clamped directly to your drawing table, but a model that rests on a floor stand is preferable. It enables you to easily change the angle of your drawing table without first removing the lamp—a feature that you should take into consideration. There are many types of lamps available, and you can check your local art supply store or look in a catalog to find one you like.

Your local art supply store may not stock all the items mentioned here, but you should be able to find equivalent ones. You can also order supplies from an art supply catalog if necessary. Just remember that in a catalog you will find other interesting items. Some are essential; others are meant only for the professional artist. Don't run out and buy all the gadgets available. There are many things in an art supply store that are quite expensive, but that you don't really need. Think carefully about what you'll need before you buy and purchase only what you will use. Limit yourself to the basics, especially if you are just beginning, and purchase the highest quality you can afford. Inexpensive art materials are not worth using, especially poor quality brushes or paper.

This is a typical studio set up. The large taboret on the left has four drawers for storage and an ample top surface for tools or reference material. There's a large waterbowl for cleaning brushes, an electric pencil sharpener, and a revolving tray that holds pencils, brushes, and ink bottles.

The carrying case to the left of the taboret contains a Polaroid 180 camera, which is helpful for shooting reference photos. The drawing table in the center has a counterbalanced board; the tilt or height can be easily adjusted. The fluorescent lamp over the table rests on a floor stand. The swivel chair is on casters and sits on a Masonite mat for ease of movement. The cabinet on the right is another storage file, while the cork board behind it provides a handy place to post sketches.

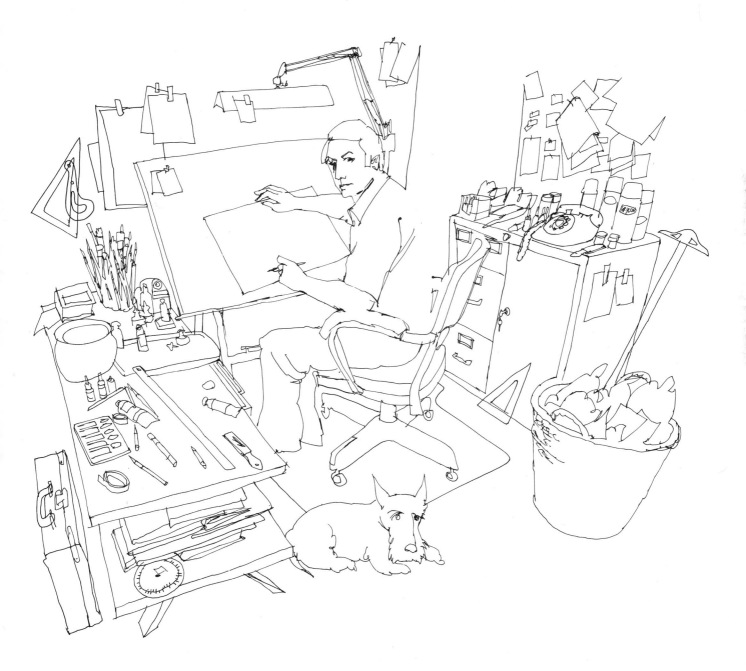

CHAPTER TWO
PENCIL EXERCISES

Familiar as you may be with the pencil in everyday life, the following discussion will show you how to prepare it for use when sketching and rendering.

SHARPENING THE PENCIL

Before beginning the exercises, take time to learn different ways to point the pencil. It takes a knack to do a good job, especially with the softer grades. Their leads are always breaking, particularly if the pencils have been previously dropped or otherwise abused.

First a word about tools to use for sharpening. There is little to recommend most pencil sharpeners, either mechanical or hand. Though they may occasionally do the job (when the lead is fairly hard or you want a very sharp point), a sharp knife or a single-edged razor blade will do a vastly superior job.

Remember, when you're ready to begin, that a pencil has a right and a wrong end to sharpen. If you whittle off the letters or numbers, it won't be easy to identify the pencil later. Start by cutting away some wood, taking care not to break the precious lead or reduce its size too much (see Figure 1). With the harder grades, you can safely expose half an inch or so, but when sharpening soft pencils—6B, 5B, 4B—you can't cut away much wood without risking immediate breakage.

Next shape the exposed lead to the desired point on a sandpaper pad or a sheet of rough paper (see Figure 2). Sometimes you may want to use both—the paper for a final slicking up after the lead has been shaped. Each time you're through using the sandpaper pad, tap it repeatedly against the rim of a wastebasket to free any loose graphite. Also wipe the pencil point with a rag or paper tissue. If graphite particles find their way to your drawing paper they can easily cause smudges.

TYPES OF POINTS

There are several types of points that you may choose depending on your purpose:

1. The first, which is the simplest to make and the most all-purpose, is shown in (1) in Figure 3. This has a uniform taper and is not unlike that made with a pencil sharpener, except that less lead is cut away and the tip is not quite so sharp. No sandpapering is required.

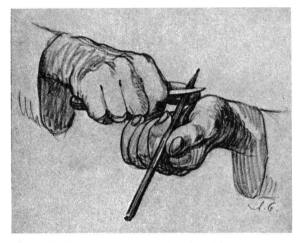

Figure 1. Start to sharpen the pencil by removing the wood. Use a sharp knife and hold it naturally.

Figure 2. Now point the lead. Position the pencil on the sandpaper depending on the type of point you want.

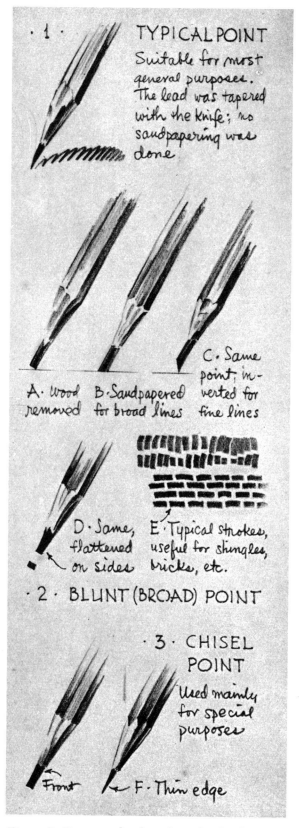

Figure 3. Here are the three basic kinds of points that you can obtain with your pencil.

2. The second type is the blunt or broad point shown in (2) in Figure 3. To make this, first cut away the wood (A), exposing a fairly long lead (except with the brittle, softest ones) all the way around. Then holding the pencil in a normal drawing position (B), rub the point on the sandpaper until it is quite blunt. After that smoothe the tip of the lead with a few strokes on the paper. This point can now be used to make either a broad or a fine stroke, depending on whether you hold the pencil in the normal drawing position (B) or inverted (C). If you wish, sandpaper the sides of the lead to create a flat point (D) that is ideal for broad, crisp individual strokes (E), which you may need for indicating square or rectangular details such as bricks, shingles, or panes of glass.

3. Some artists like what is known as a "chisel point," which is sandpapered on two sides to produce a thin edge (3). This can be used to draw either a fine or a broad line, depending on how it is held, or it may be manipulated to form a stroke that varies in character throughout its length. One disadvantage is that this point breaks easily.

Artists do most work with the medium or blunt point (1), which is how the point wears naturally, and only prepare a special point for some particular purpose. The main thing is to always use the type of point—as well as the degree of lead—that you think will best serve your need at the moment. As you work through the following exercises, try all sorts of points and you will eventually learn the capabilities of each one.

HOLDING THE PENCIL

How you position your hand depends on how you place your paper—whether it's vertical, sloping steeply, or nearly flat—and on the technical requirements of your drawing—whether it calls for sweeping strokes, carefully executed lines, or what. For typical work, most artists hold the pencil as if they were writing, with the hand resting lightly on the table, as shown in (1) in Figure 4, though they use the pencil with far greater freedom. For short strokes and strokes demanding considerable pressure, you need little arm movement. Swing the hand at the wrist, or let the fingers alone perform the necessary motions. For longer strokes—ones that are quick and dashing—hold the pencil well back from the point, and swing the entire forearm and hand freely from the elbow, with a minimum of wrist and finger movement, as shown in (2).

For particularly unrestrained effort, such as that required to quickly block in construction lines of a subject (especially if you're working at an easel or on a large-scale drawing), hold the pencil (which should preferably be full length) with the unsharpened end in your palm (3) and swing your hand and write very boldly. You may even invert your hand (4), which permits amazingly rapid progress.

For most shaded work, the quality of line and tone desired will determine your hand position, which may change frequently. Occasionally, you may want to keep the pencil almost vertical (5). This position sometimes proves useful when you want to build up tone very carefully with a sharp point.

Eventually try all positions.

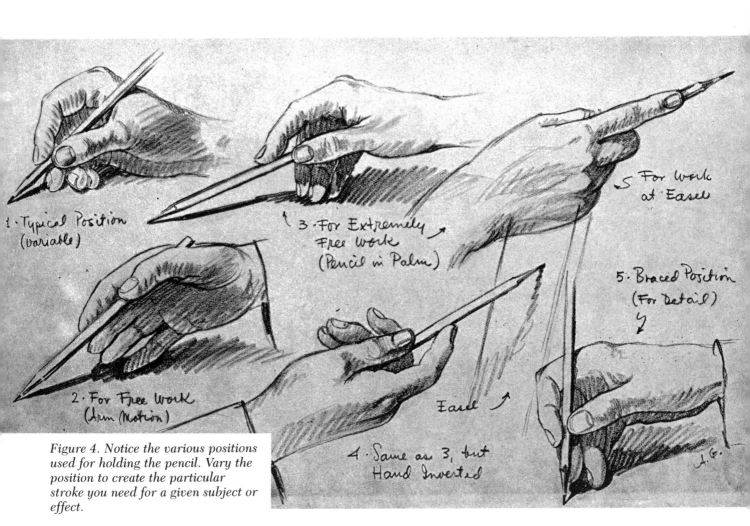

1. Typical Position
(Variable)

2. For Free Work
(Arm Motion)

3. For Extremely
Free Work
(Pencil in Palm)

4. Same as 3, but
Hand Inverted

Easel

5 For Work
at Easel

5. Braced Position
(For Detail)

Figure 4. Notice the various positions used for holding the pencil. Vary the position to create the particular stroke you need for a given subject or effect.

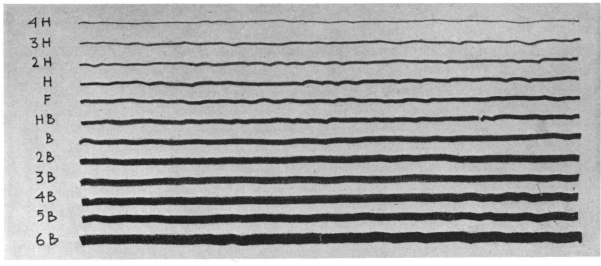

4 H
3 H
2 H
H
F
HB
B
2 B
3 B
4 B
5 B
6 B

Figure 5. Different pencils produce different results.

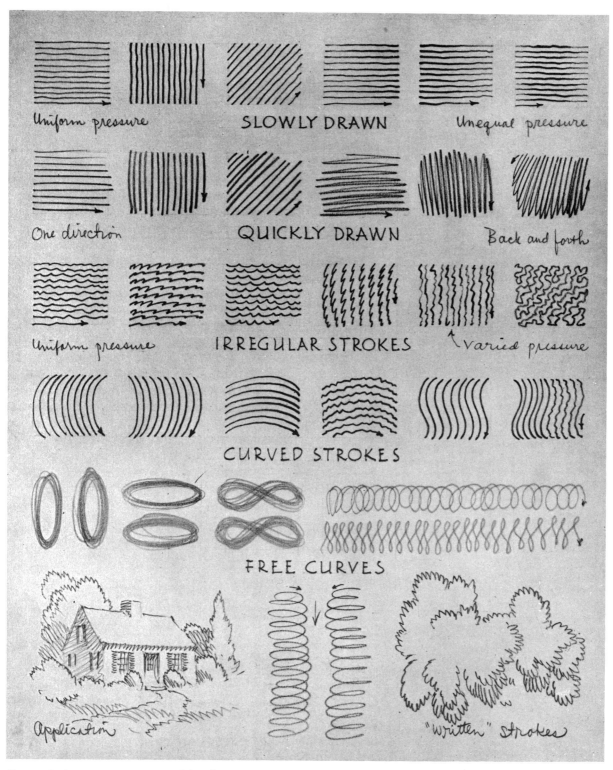

Uniform pressure   SLOWLY DRAWN   Unequal pressure

One direction   QUICKLY DRAWN   Back and forth

Uniform pressure   IRREGULAR STROKES   Varied pressure

CURVED STROKES

FREE CURVES

Application   "written" strokes

Figure 6. An amazing variety of fine lines is possible. Make pages and pages of strokes, using all your pencils.

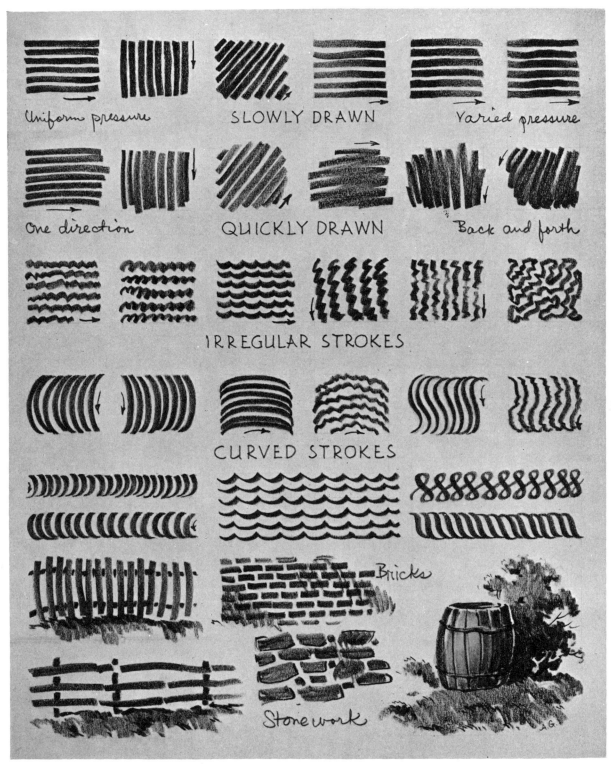

Uniform pressure SLOWLY DRAWN Varied pressure

One direction QUICKLY DRAWN Back and forth

IRREGULAR STROKES

CURVED STROKES

Bricks

Stonework

Figure 7. The most natural strokes are usually the best. Copy these strokes freely and invent others of your own.

PRACTICING LINES

Because the pencil is primarily a linear tool, a good starting point is to experiment by drawing lines—hundreds of lines of all kinds: long and short; fine, medium, and broad; straight, crooked, curved; broken and unbroken; dots and dashes. Try every grade of pencil and different papers. Vary the pressure too, as well as hand position and speed.

Figures 5, 6, and 7 show ways to practice linework. Try these lines and invent others of your own. You should experiment until you discover every type of line each pencil is capable of making. Begin with the sharpest point, and then try broader and broader ones, ending with the full-sized lead shown in Figure 5.

Although the examples in the figures were reproduced at the exact size of the originals, do at least part of your work at a larger scale and with greater boldness. Try drawing lines ranging from 1″ to 6″ (3 to 15 cm). Sweep some strokes still longer, letting some of these take the natural curve that the swing of the arm encourages. Draw others as straight as you can.

Flip through the book and copy a few lines here and there, remembering that most of the illustrations have been reduced considerably from the originals. If you have access to any pencil drawings see how closely you can imitate the individual strokes.

With these exercises you will gradually come to a fuller appreciation of the pencil's possibilities, while developing your own technical repertoire. Eventually you will make, almost unconsciously, the type of stroke every purpose demands.

TONE-BUILDING EXERCISES

Once you have thoroughly tested all your pencils as linear instruments, experiment to see how many varieties of gray and black tones you can produce with them.

Two Types of Tones. Fundamentally, there are only two types of tones: those where the component pencil lines (or dots) are so merged that their individual identity is wholly or largely lost and those where at least some lines (or dots) are plainly visible. Tones of the first type are called "true" tones. An example is shown in (1) in Figure 8, where the area has been repeatedly gone over in different directions with fine strokes until all traces of line have disappeared.

The second type of tone is shown in (2). It consists of lines so closely grouped that you are conscious—particularly if you view the area from a distance—of a tonal, rather than a linear, impression. Such a tone is called "illusory," in that it is only an illusion of tone, since the eye creates a tonal impression by automatically blending (to some extent) the dark lines and the white spaces between them.

Another illusory tone is shown in (3); here closely spaced dots are merged by the eye. Short dashes, if close enough together, can also create a tonal effect of this basic type.

In pencil drawing, all such tones—and there is an infinite variety of them—can be used according to your needs and often in combination. You should therefore experiment with every method of creating tone that occurs to you. The examples in Figure 8 typify both the solid and linear (or dotted) kinds.

Flat and Graded Tones. For some purposes, tones that are uniform throughout—"flat" or "ungraded," as they are known—are preferable. Other subjects may call for "graded" or "graduated" tones in which the amount of light or dark varies by degrees from part to part. More rarely, you may need "hit-or-miss" tones that follow no set pattern. Note the decorative tones in Figure 9. Graded tones will be discussed in more detail in Chapter 4, "Creating Tones and Rendering," on page 25.

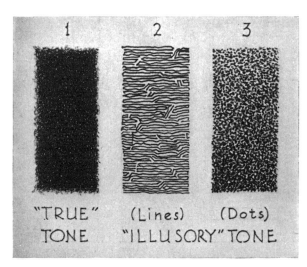

Figure 8. There are two basic types of tones: "true" tones made by strokes of the pencil and "illusory" tones built up from pencil lines or dots.

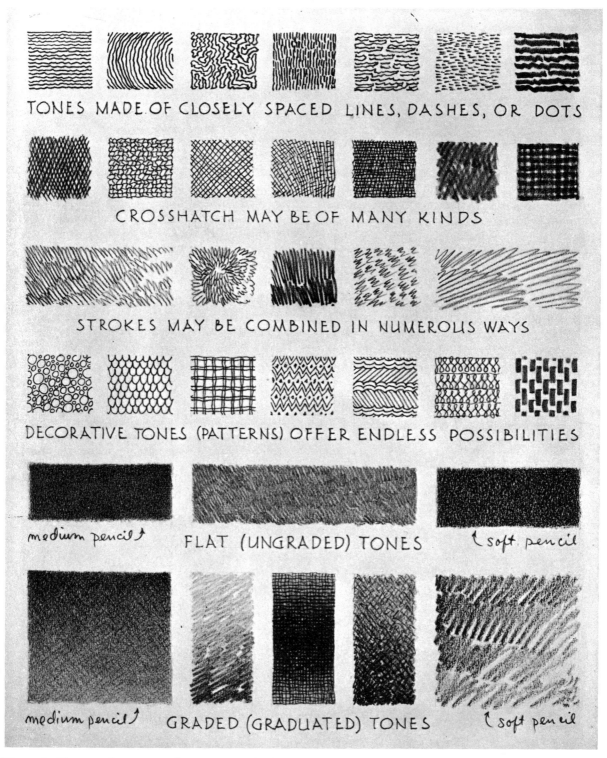

TONES MADE OF CLOSELY SPACED LINES, DASHES, OR DOTS

CROSSHATCH MAY BE OF MANY KINDS

STROKES MAY BE COMBINED IN NUMEROUS WAYS

DECORATIVE TONES (PATTERNS) OFFER ENDLESS POSSIBILITIES

medium pencil↗   FLAT (UNGRADED) TONES   ↙soft pencil

medium pencil↗   GRADED (GRADUATED) TONES   ↙soft pencil

Figure 9. The pencil is a versatile instrument for building tone.

CHAPTER THREE
PEN AND BRUSH EXERCISES

Drawing with a pen or brush may be difficult at first, but with a little practice you'll learn to control these tools and become familiar with what they can and cannot do. Just as you once learned to write the alphabet by practicing the formation of letters, you'll learn to draw by practicing lines and textures that in combination can represent specific objects, such as grass, wood, trees, or concrete.

There are an extraordinary number of drawing styles and methods that you can use when drawing in ink. You can develop a very personal style, as distinct as your own handwriting. In fact, many artists have developed styles that are easily recognizable even when their drawings aren't signed.

It's very important that you practice drawing every day if possible—which is as often as you would practice, for example, if you were learning how to play the piano. If you do this, drawing with the pen and brush will come to feel very natural,

the way writing is now. And as you become more familiar and comfortable with the tools, you'll gain the confidence that will help you improve and grow as an artist.

The pen and brush have certain limitations that can be learned only by practicing on different illustration boards and paper surfaces. Certain boards have textures that can limit the freedom of your drawing strokes. While the pen may catch on the surface and cause a splatter on a rough surface, the brush will give you great freedom on the same paper. On the other hand, on a very slick and smooth surface, the pen will glide along with ease. If you do pen drawings on a slightly textured surface, however, being conscious of the possibility of the pen snagging on the surface may make you draw more carefully.

Most pen points offer varying degrees of flexibility, resulting in a wide range of line weights (see examples on pages 20–24). Some points are

extremely flexible and capable of a remarkable range of line weights, while others are very stiff, producing an even, uniform line. The technical drawing pen also produces an even line because its point is actually a small tube. Its great advantage is that you can draw in any direction on most surfaces without the point catching.

Brushes are also versatile drawing tools that offer a great variation in linear quality. With a well-pointed brush, you can draw both fine and bold lines. To draw a very bold line the brush must be fully loaded with ink. If this brush is flattened and used with a small amount of ink, it can create a unique dry-brush effect.

The following exercises in this chapter are designed to help you become confident using the pen and brush. Try to practice at least one or two hours a day and you'll soon gain the control needed to become proficient with these tools.

EXERCISE 1. SHAPES AND LINES

To loosen up, begin by writing with a crowquill pen on a piece of plate-finish bristol board. Then practice drawing various shapes and lines—both fine and heavy as shown. Since the plate-finish board is very smooth, the possibility of the pen snagging the surface is minimized. See what range of line weights you can produce with this particular point.

Draw both fast and very slowly, and notice the different line quality. Bear down lightly and then draw using more pressure on the pen point. Hold the pen in a variety of positions and take note of the different results. A little practice like this and you'll learn how the crowquill pen reacts to this particular paper surface. When you finish, try the same thing on other board and paper surfaces.

Here the crowquill pen is being used as for writing. Note how many line variations and textures can be made with the pen in this position—and try it yourself.

The position of the pen is changed here, and therefore it is producing a different kind of line. Note how the pen is being stroked sideways quickly to draw a series of lines.

also practice writing with the crowquill pen....

EXERCISE 2. LINES AND TEXTURES

Practice drawing groups of lines and textures, such as the ones here, first with a pen and then with a brush. Try a variety of pens and brushes to see how they differ.

Very quickly done; drawn with an even pressure.

Lines drawn slowly, moving the pen up and down slightly.

Same as above, but using more pressure on the point.

Lines of different weights drawn using a zigzag motion.

Drawn with a nervous motion and even pressure.

Varying the pressure on the point.

Lines formed by drawing short overlapping strokes.

Series of small loops.

Various dotted or broken lines.

Quickly drawn brush lines.

Slowly drawn brush lines.

Zigzag brush lines.

Lines using more pressure on the brush tip.

Loose, short brushstrokes forming a scratchy line.

Brush line drawn with a nervous motion.

Split brush line.

EXERCISE 3. PEN LINES

Now concentrate on all sorts of pen lines, experimenting with spacing, pressure on the point, and curves. Of the nine groups of lines shown here, draw the first lines (at the top or left of the square) straight, uniform, and evenly spaced. Draw the next lines closer together; the ones following as close to each other as possible without touching; next, nervous and scratchy lines; nervous, scratchy lines drawn with more pressure; and finally (at the bottom or on the right of the square) loose random lines.

Horizontal lines.

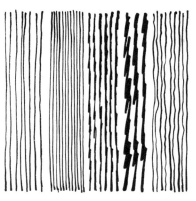

Vertical lines.

Varying the pressure on the point.

Controlling line weights.

Lines of varying weights created by increasing pressure on the point.

Quickly drawn lines of different weights.

Vertical strokes drawn by varying pressure on the point.

Curved lines drawn slowly.

Curved lines drawn very quickly.

EXERCISE 4. RULING WITH A PEN AND BRUSH

Ruling with the pen is a very useful technique. Try drawing first thin and then heavier lines by varying the pressure on the pen point—try to duplicate the lines illustrated here. After a while, use a brush; this is a little harder to do and you may find it quite difficult at first. Rest the ferrule of the brush against the ruler and very carefully draw a straight line, maintaining an even pressure on the point.

To rule with a pen, rest the pen against the ruler and carefully draw a line applying even pressure on the pen point. With a little practice, you'll gain the control needed to draw in this manner. Note that you can also do this with a brush.

Series of pen lines in an even tone ruled closely together.

Slightly heavier pen lines. More pressure is used, but it is evenly maintained.

Pen lines gradually drawn heavier. Very heavy ones made by overlapping.

Pen lines ruled by varying the pressure on the point.

A nervous motion with the pen creates a texture.

Series of lines in an even tone ruled closely together with a brush.

Slightly heavier brush lines, drawn with more pressure.

Brush lines gradually drawn heavier.

Lines ruled by varying the pressure on the brush point.

Brush lines ruled using a nervous motion to create a texture.

EXERCISE 5. BRUSH LINES

These brush exercises are the same as those suggested for the pen in Exercise 3. Practice them many times until you can do them with ease. Be sure to use a high-quality red sable brush—#2 or #3—or you'll have problems. Cheaper brushes either won't maintain a good point or will split, making it impossible to draw fine lines.

Horizontal lines.

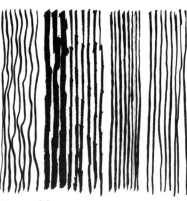

Vertical lines.

Varying the pressure on the point.

Controlling line weights.

Lines of varying weights created by increasing pressure on the brush point.

Quickly drawn lines of different weights.

Vertical brushstrokes drawn by varying the pressure on the point.

Curved lines drawn slowly.

Curved lines drawn very quickly.

CHAPTER FOUR
CREATING TONES AND RENDERING

Herbert S. Kates

In art the word "value" refers to the relative amount of light or dark in some given area. If an object is light in color or tone, for instance, it is said to be light in value; if dark, it's said to be dark in value. An essential skill is knowing how to create values or tones to give feeling and impact to your drawings and renderings.

OBTAINING TONES IN PEN DRAWING

If you want to represent an object that is light in value, you usually draw tones that are also light in value. For example, if you want to show a dark apple against a light yellow background you use values of dark and light closely approximating the amount of dark and light in the objects themselves. Because of the technical limitations of the pen, however—which make it difficult to show all the possible range of values from the white of the paper to the black of the ink—you often have to simplify actual values when you draw them. Light objects, for instance, are often shown as white and dark ones as black. If objects have a large number of slightly varying tones, they can be simplified and only the general ones expressed.

Notice the delightful sketch by Herbert S. Kates heading this chapter. Very few values have been used, yet the whole is most effective. The simplicity of the handling is consistent with the plainness of the architecture.

In drawing it is not the absolute correctness of each tone, however, that is most important (though accuracy is helpful), but it is the right arrangement of the various values that is essential. It is easy to make objects "out of value" in relation to their surroundings even though they may seem good individually. So if you learn to express individual values now, you will soon use this knowledge almost unconsciously, no matter the media or the materials. That way your mind will be free to cope with the other dynamics of drawing and composition.

MAKING VALUE SCALES

To start practicing values, make several scales similar to that shown in (1) in Figure 1 or in Figures 2, 3, and 4. In Figure 1 the upper rectangular space in (1) indicates the white. The black on the bottom was drawn next. In the middle gray notice that the black lines are approximately the same widths as the white spaces left between them. This middle value is truly halfway between the black and the white. The light gray is supposed to be halfway between the white and the middle gray and the dark gray halfway between the middle gray and the black. The whole scale thus gives a natural gradation from the white to the black.

Unfortunately, the light gray in this value scale seems to show too sudden a change from the white. This is largely an optical effect due to the

strongly contrasting margin lines around it, as well as to the darkening tendency that the black margins have on the light gray tone.

Figure 2 is better in this respect. Copy this scale, keeping the tones next to each other as shown. In this sketch there is no pure white or black, only a graded scale of five values. The change in value is created by adding lines to each unit of tone and by slightly widening the lines by increasing pressure on the pen as the dark is approached.

In Figure 3 crosshatching is used to produce similar tonal results. Figure 4 shows a somewhat freer type of technique used in much the same way. If you look in Figure 1 at the value scale in (3) you can see that it is possible to form areas of almost any desired tone even with definite patterns of decorative effects.

BUILDING GRAY VALUES

Once you have made a number of these scales [you may add tones showing a wider range of values if you wish, for instance, by adding one between each pair shown in (1) of Figure 1], try experimenting by representing portions of objects of neutral color in the correct value. Take a bit of gray paper, for example, and try to produce in ink on your white drawing paper the correct effect of the value of the gray. Or take a white cardboard box and build a gray corresponding to some portion of the box as it appears grayed by shade or

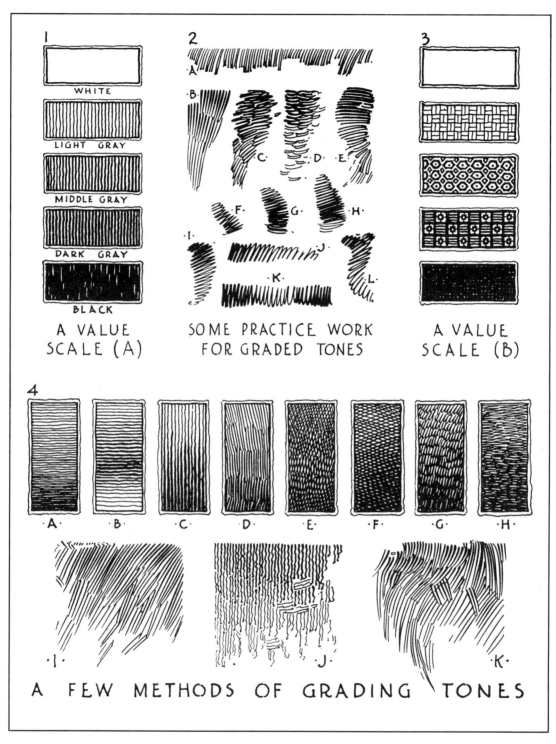

A VALUE SCALE (A)

SOME PRACTICE WORK FOR GRADED TONES

A VALUE SCALE (B)

WHITE

LIGHT GRAY

MIDDLE GRAY

DARK GRAY

BLACK

A FEW METHODS OF GRADING TONES

Figure 1. Here are four methods of obtaining values and grading tones. It's important to practice these exercises.

In (1) a value scale gives a natural gradation from white on the top to black on the bottom. In the middle gray the black lines are approximately the same widths as the white spaces left between them—truly halfway between the black and the white. The light gray is halfway between the white and the middle gray and the dark gray halfway between the middle gray and the black.

In (2) there are a number of free-stroke combinations running from light to dark or dark to light. Experiment making many varieties.

In (3) note that it is possible to form areas of almost any desired tone even with definite patterns of decorative effects.

In (4) there is a group of more carefully constructed tones (A through H), each of which is graded to some extent. In (A) lines of uniform width have been placed more closely together until they finally merge into a nearly solid black. At (B) the pen pressure is varied so that the weight of the strokes is gradually increased and then decreased to shade the tone. An example of tapering lines used in juxtaposition is shown in (C). Tones in (D through H) are easily created, while larger areas in (I through K) are graded with more freedom.

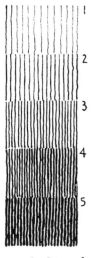
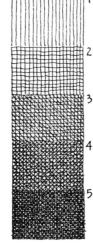
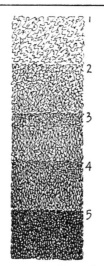

Figure 2. Copy this value scale, placing one tone directly against the next. Notice that neither pure white nor any solid black appears at either extreme of the scale.

Figure 3. Cross-hatching may be used to indicate a value scale.

Figure 4. This value scale is even freer in treatment and no less effective.

Figure 5. It is not necessary to separate tonal areas completely in order to suggest change.

Figure 6. A variety of strokes may be used to obtain similar effects.

Figure 7. Graded tones are indicated here with free-form strokes.

Figure 8. Here values are indicated by increasing the width of the horizontal strokes.

shadow. (Don't draw the box; just indicate a small area of its tone.)

When dealing with grays, whose relative values are *perceived* without difficulty, the problem is mainly one of *representing* those values. When objects are in color, however, it takes some skill for the artist to perceive them correctly and then translate or interpret them in terms of value. As an aid in determining the correct value of any object—whether neutral or color—it is helpful to compare the surface with some white object (a sheet of white paper will do nicely) that is exposed to the maximum available light. You will find that many objects of different colors may have the same value, while objects with the same color and value may vary greatly depending on differences in lighting.

GRADING TONES

Up to this point you have practiced tones that are uniformly gray. But since many objects show gradations of tone, you must become proficient in grading tones. Start building graded tones as soon as you feel skilled at handling flat ones.

The group of flat tones in Figure 2 gives something of a graded effect, but it lacks smoothness. It takes only a step from this, however, to make the graded tones shown in Figures 5 through 8. Practice tones like these.

Figure 1 also shows other ways to grade tones. In (2) there are a number of free stroke combinations running from light to dark or from dark to light; you should experiment making as many varieties as possible.

In (4) there is a group of more carefully constructed tones (A through H), each of which is graded to some extent. In (A) lines of uniform width have been placed more closely together toward the bottom until finally they merge. At (B) the pen pressure is varied so that the weight of the strokes is gradually increased and then decreased. An example of tapering lines is shown in (C). Tones in (D through H) are created easily, while larger areas are graded more freely in (I through K).

Innumerable combinations similar to these are possible. Try as many of them as you wish, so after this you will have the dexterity needed to allow you to proceed rapidly with the exercises that follow.

EXERCISE 1. TONAL VALUE WITH A PEN

Experiment with the pen to explore tonal values created by straight, crosshatching, and zigzag lines.

At the top are short, vertical strokes, while at the center strokes are drawn with more pressure. At the bottom, lines are drawn closely together—lighter on left, darker on right.

At the top vertical strokes with horizontal lines drawn over them create a crosshatched effect; at the bottom the same technique is used with heavier lines.

Lines drawn first closely together and then gradually farther apart produce a gradation of tone at the top. At the bottom a gradation is achieved with crosshatching.

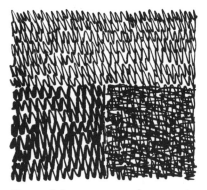

Up-and-down pen strokes are drawn closely together at the top. At the bottom left a darker tone is created with a heavier zigzag line, while at the bottom right is a crosshatched zigzag.

Here are three examples of graduated strokes: top, very short; middle, longer dash; and bottom, zigzag lines.

Different effects can be achieved with crosshatching: top left, a basic pattern; top right, another pattern over the first; center, crosshatching with more pressure; bottom, graduated lines.

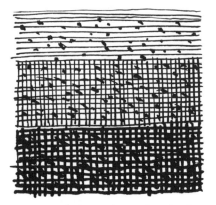

Here straight and crosshatched lines with dots are drawn to create a unique texture.

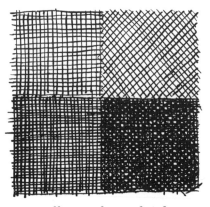

More effects with crosshatching are shown here: top left, even pattern; top right, 45° angle; bottom left, a heavier but even line; and bottom right, top two patches drawn a little heavier over one another.

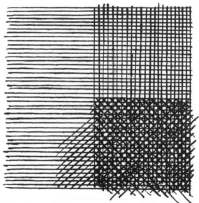

In the whole square lines have been ruled horizontally with a pen, while at the top right lines have also been drawn horizontally and at the bottom right two sets of lines at 45° angles have been added.

EXERCISE 2. MORE PEN LINES AND TEXTURES

Here are some more combinations of lines and textures for you to practice. On the left is a series of graduated tones. With the white, the black, and the four grays in between you can draw almost anything. Remember the white can be the paper or board. By simply varying the line weights, you can produce any number of intermediate gray tones.

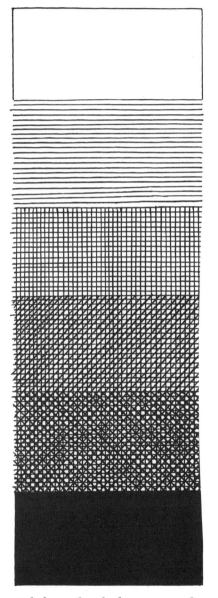  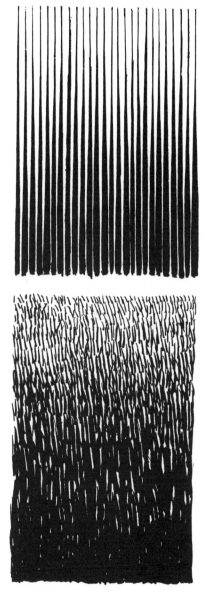

Ruled crosshatched pen tones of different values are shown from top to bottom; the white of the board; light horizontal lines; vertical lines drawn over the horizontal ones; sets of lines drawn over the first two sets at a 45° angle; lines drawn at a 45° angle from the other direction; solid black.

Loosely drawn, random crosshatched lines are graduated from light to solid black.

At the top a graduated tone is created by ruling lines of varying weight closely together. At the bottom short pen strokes are graduated from light to solid black.

CHAPTER FIVE
FREEHAND PERSPECTIVE

As you study perspective you will soon discover that objects appear different in shape from what you know them to be. For instance, you know that a cube has six equal faces and that each of them is a square. Yet if you draw six squares, combining them in any and every possible way, the final result will in no way suggest a cube.

Another example is the cylinder. You know that the top of an upright cylinder is a circle, but you seldom see it as a true circle unless you look straight at the end. It actually appears elliptical or even as a straight line. Yet you think of it as a circle simply because you know it is one, not because it really looks circular.

So when you question how something should be drawn, you must study not only the things themselves, but also the science of perspective. This science gives principles that are helpful in drawing objects correctly— not as they actually are, but as they appear from the point at which they are viewed. Freehand perspective trains you to apply these principles to the practical problems of freehand sketching.

For the purposes of this book only a few of the more important principles will be briefly discussed. Nothing short of a complete text could do justice to the subject, and there are already many excellent works available. In addition to your reading on the subject, learn to observe the perspective appearance of objects all around you. If you are studying circles and ellipses, for instance, notice every circular arch, clock face, waste basket, or other familiar forms you see every day.

TWO IMPORTANT PRINCIPLES

There are only a few fundamental principles of perspective. The following two are the most important:

1. The apparent size of an object decreases in proportion to its distance from an imaginary plane that passes through the eye at right angles to the direction in which you are looking.

2. A surface appears in its true shape only when parallel to the picture plane or, in other words, when at right angles to the line of sight from eye to surface.

The first principle can be easily tested if you stand close to a window and look straight through it. An entire building in the distance appears only a few inches or several centimeters large. If there are several objects of equal size at varying distances from your eye, you will notice that the nearest one appears to be the largest and the others seem smaller and smaller in proportion to their distance away from you.

The second principle is also easy to demonstrate. When a surface (take a circular end of a cylinder, for example) is not placed at right angles to the line of sight, the dimension that is turned away appears smaller. The farther it is turned, the smaller this dimension seems, until it is turned so far that the surface coincides with the direction of sight, causing it to appear simply as a line. This apparent change of shape is called "foreshortening."

TYPICAL GEOMETRIC FORMS

For you to gain a quick, direct working knowledge of these princi-ples, a few typical geometric forms will be discussed here. Once you understand the simple forms it won't be difficult for you to draw more complex objects by simply applying the exact same principles to them.

Horizon Line or Eye Level. The horizon line is an imaginary horizontal line at eye level. When drawing objects or other small work, the latter term is commonly used; for buildings and outdoor work in general, the former is usually used.

The appearance of any object will vary according to whether it is at, above, or to the left of the viewer. To observe the variations that occur when viewing objects from various points, take simple objects and hold them in different positions, noticing how they look when moved from place to place, nearer or farther from the eye and higher or lower in relation to the horizon line.

The Sphere. Take, for example, an orange, an apple, or some other spherical object. When held above the eye, it appears as a circle. Below the eye and at eye level, its contour is practically the same. If it is a true sphere there will not be the slightest variation no matter where you hold it.

Although a sphere remains the same in profile regardless of its posi-tion, you see different portions of its surface as it is moved up and down, shifted to the right or left, or spun round and round. Figure 1 illustrates this point. Study this and then draw several spherical objects placed in a variety of positions.

Bear in mind that you seldom see

halfway around a sphere. Figure 2 explains this clearly.

The Vertical Cylinder. Now take a cylinder—a paper tube will do—and hold it vertically. With one eye closed, raise it until the top is level with the other eye. In this position the top circle will appear as a straight line, the circular plane being so much foreshortened that only its edge can be seen.

Now lower it a bit. The circular top is now visible, but it is still so foreshortened that it appears elliptical instead of circular. Lower it still farther and the ellipse becomes rounder. Just as this top ellipse appears more rounded as it is dropped below the eye, so if the bottom of the cylinder were fully seen, it would appear even rounder than the top, as it is still farther below the eye. Experience proves that the degree of roundness of the ellipse is in proportion to its distance below the eye.

Next raise the cylinder vertically until the lower end is at eye level. This now appears as a straight line, just as the top end did before. Raise it still higher and the bottom comes in sight as an ellipse; the top of the cylinder is now hidden. And the higher the cylinder is raised, the rounder the ellipse of the bottom becomes, its fullness in proportion to its distance above eye level. If the cylinder is lowered until the bottom and top are both equidistant from eye level, both will be visible. But the visible edges of each will have a similar curvature. (What is true of the appearance of the top or bottom of a cylinder in perspective is true of any circle.)

The cylinder, when held vertically, will appear symmetrical about a vertical axis line at all times, every element of the cylindrical surface also being vertical. Like the sphere, you seldom see halfway around the circumference. Less than half the cylindrical surface is visible at any one time.

Now try a number of sketches of the vertical cylinder and the horizontal circle as viewed from different positions—Figure 3 shows you a few. Also practice drawing ellipses until you can do them well; this is no easy matter. (The tipped or horizontal cylinder will be discussed later in this chapter.)

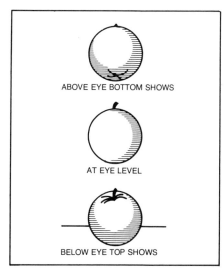

Figure 1. The sphere remains the same in profile regardless of its position. However, if you take an apple with the stem at the top and hold it upright, but below the eye, not only is the stem visible, so is a portion of the surface beyond it. If you raise it until the top of the apple is at eye level, still holding it upright, you still see the stem, but none of the surface beyond is visible. A bit of the "blossom" below may now show.

As you raise it above the eye the stem will gradually disappear, as well as a portion of the top surface. As this is lost to view, more of the lower part will become visible, so if it is held some distance above the eye you will see the entire "blossom" and the surface beyond.

You see different portions of a sphere's surface as it is moved up and down, shifted to the right or left, or spun round and round. Study this illustration and then draw several spherical objects placed in a variety of positions.

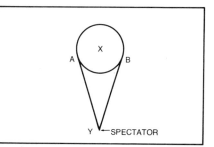

Figure 2. You seldom see halfway around a sphere. For example, if X represents the top view of the sphere and Y the position of the viewer, the lines drawn from Y tangent to the sphere (A and B) mark the limits of the visible portion of the sphere at the place of its greatest circumference. The larger the sphere or the closer the viewer, the smaller this distance becomes.

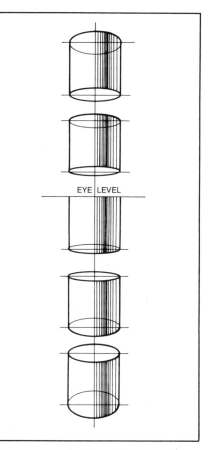

Figure 3. Study these characteristics of the vertical cylinder and the horizontal circle, and try a number of sketches from different positions.

The Vertical Cone. While you still have the horizontal circle in mind, consider the circular cone placed vertically. Figure 4 shows the cone in this position. Notice that the appearance of the circle is the same as in the case of the cylinder. If the apex of the cone is at the top and the cone is below the eye, you can see more than halfway around the conical surface. If the cone is raised above the eye, you see less than halfway around. And if the cone is inverted, the opposite is true. Note also that a circular cone will always appear symmetrical, the long axis of the ellipse of the base being at right angles to the axis of the cone. Make several drawings of the vertical cone. (The horizontal or tipped cone will be discussed later.)

The Cube in Parallel Perspective. Now look at the cube. Hold it with the top at eye level and the nearer face at right angles to the line of sight so you can see its true shape. Only one face of the cube is visible now, and that appears as a square. Lower the cube a few inches or centimeters and the top appears, greatly foreshortened. The farther horizontal edge, being a greater distance away than the nearer one, seems shorter. The parallel receding edges of the top seem to slant. If these slanting edges were continued indefinitely, they would appear to meet at a certain point, and that point would be at eye level.

Lower the cube a few inches or centimeters farther. The top now appears wider and the two receding edges have still greater slant. If continued they would still meet at a point at eye level, the same one as before. The front face still appears square.

Now raise the cube above the eye, still holding it vertically. The top goes out of sight and the bottom becomes visible. The front face looks square as before. Now the higher the cube is raised, the more the bottom shows. The receding lines now seem to slant downward toward eye level. If continued they would meet at the very same point on eye level as when the cube was below the eye.

To convince yourself that these same facts are true of other objects, take a box or anything similar to the cube, and study it in various horizontal positions above and below the eye, keeping the nearest vertical plane so turned that it is always seen in its true shape.

It is interesting to note, as mentioned above, that the receding parallel edges would, if continued far enough, appear to converge toward the same point at eye level, exactly opposite the eye itself. This point is called the "vanishing point" for that set of edges. The edges that do not recede do not appear to converge and hence have no vanishing point.

When an object like the cube or box is placed in such a way that its principal face is at right angles to the line of sight from the eye, it is said to be viewed in "parallel perspective." Figure 5 shows cubes in parallel perspective in various relations to eye level.

The Cube in Angular Perspective. Now turn the cube to a new position, placing it horizontally below the eye and turned at an angle with all four of its top edges receding. None of the edges now appears horizontal.

Note that if the cube is turned in such a way to make equal angles with the line of sight as at (A) in Figure 6, you will see equal portions of the lines marked *a* and *b*, and they will have an equal slant. The same will be true of *c* and *d*. Now if you turn the cube so that it makes unequal angles with the line of sight as at (B), the line *a* will seem shorter and line *b* longer than before.

To more firmly fix these concepts, shift the cube from place to place and ask yourself: If two edges of the square top of the cube recede from me at unequal angles, which of the two appears longer? Which is more nearly horizontal?

If you continue your analysis in this thorough way you will observe many interesting things. You will see that the edges of the cube that are truly vertical appear that way and therefore should be drawn that way. Note also that the nearest vertical edge will be

the longest and that the others will decrease in length as they get farther away.

When a cube or other object is placed so that no surface is seen in its true shape or that its principal planes are at other than a right angle with the line of sight, it is said to be in "angular perspective." Because it is rather difficult for the beginner to draw angular perspective well, it is better to work for some time from a cube itself, placing it in different positions above and below the eye. To draw such an object, it is usually advisable to locate and actually draw a line representing eye level on paper, making sure that the various receding lines are converging to the proper vanishing points on this eye level. It is sometimes wise in these early problems to actually continue such receding lines indefinitely, allowing them to meet at the proper

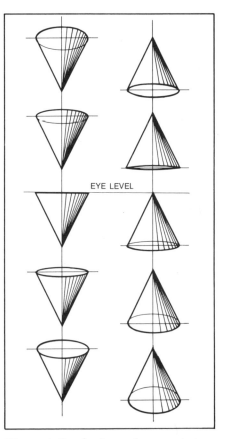

Figure 4. Study these characteristics of the vertical cone. Notice that the appearance of the circle is the same as of the cylinder.

points, as at C and D in Figure 6.

What counts most in drawing all these objects is observation and practice based on observing the things themselves.

The Horizontal Cylinder. Now that you have a little knowledge of receding lines, go back to the cylinder. Only this time don't place it vertically. Hold it instead in a horizontal position at the level of one eye (closing the other) and turn it so that the circular end appears in its true shape.

In this position you can see nothing but the end. If you then swing it or tip it so that the end and some of the curved surface are both visible, the end will appear as an ellipse. The less curved surface that shows, the rounder this ellipse will be. Then swing the cylinder until one end appears as a straight line. In this

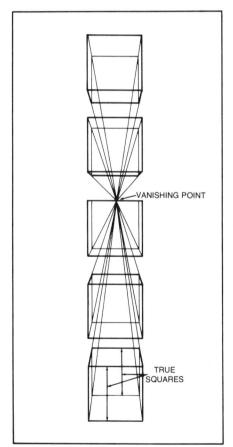

Figure 5. Observe the cube in parallel perspective in various relations to eye level.

position the other end is invisible, but if the cylinder were transparent, this end would appear as an ellipse.

Study the cylinder in all sorts of positions above and below the eye, as shown in Figure 7.

The Tipped Cone. Turning to the cone for further consideration, look directly at its apex and you will find that it appears as a true circle. When held in such a way that its base becomes a straight line, it has the contour of a triangle.

The visible curved surface of a cone may range from all to none of it. The boundaries of the cone are always represented by straight lines tangent to the ellipse, which represents the base. And the cone, like the cylinder, will always appear symmetrical, being divided by its long axis into two equal parts.

Study the sketches of cylinders and cones in Figure 7 and then make many of your own.

Other Geometric Forms. In just the same way, consider other geometric forms, such as the triangular prism placed vertically and horizontally, as well as the pyramid and hexagonal prism placed in various positions. Though a full discussion isn't possible here, a few facts about the appearance of the triangle, the hexagon, and so on are worth noting. But first let's discuss the square in greater detail in Figure 8 and the hexagon in Figure 9.

In drawing polygons, especially regular ones such as the hexagon, it is often easiest to first draw an ellipse representing a circumscribed circle. In drawing a decagonal prism, for instance, first draw an ellipse just as for the cylinders, and then draw the decagon within it. Try a number of polygons and later prisms and pyramids built upon polygonal bases.

Concentric Circles. Even in so brief a discussion on perspective, it is necessary to refer to concentric circles because they are frequently drawn and often cause trouble. Students sometimes are under the mistaken impression that circles in perspective do not appear as true

ellipses. They argue that since the nearer half of the ellipse is not as far from the viewer as the other half, it appears larger and hence must be drawn so. Although this may sound logical, it is not true. If you test actual objects, you'll find that circles always appear in perspective as true ellipses. To make this clear, refer to Figure 10.

When you feel able to do all the more common geometric forms individually in every possible position, combine several of them. After sufficient practice, apply the same principles to drawing objects of all sorts and sizes based on the same forms. And as you draw, analyze and memorize. Also try freehand perspective sketches from memory or imagination.

ARCHITECTURAL EXAMPLES

Once you have gained skill in drawing simple forms, it's not difficult to apply that knowledge to more complex subjects. Let's consider, for example, drawing buildings.

Assume that you are to draw a house 20' [6 meters (m)] wide, 40' (12 m) long, and 20' (6 m) from the ground to the eaves, with the house turned so that you look more directly at the long face than at the end. Assume that the land is level. Such a house is shown in Figure 11.

You may feel that the conditions shown in Figure 11 are idealized conditions—that few houses would be the proportion of two cubes—and this is true. It isn't difficult, however, with a cube drawn as a unit, to add one or several more cubes or even a portion of one in any direction. If the house just drawn was to be 30' (9 m) long, for instance, instead of 40' (12 m), the second cube could be easily cut in half. Either the correct perspective distance could be judged by eye, or the diagonals of its nearest face could be crossed, which would give the correct point of intersection for the cut.

Once the main proportions are established, the doors and windows, roof overhangs, and so on can be added. You will learn through experience many uses for diagonal lines—for instance, locating centers, mea-

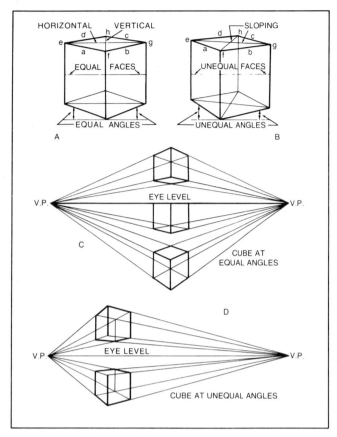

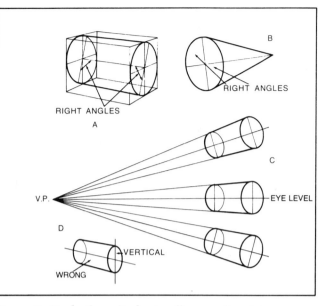

Figure 6. Study the cube as it appears in angular perspective. Note that if the cube is turned in such a way to make equal angles with the line of sight as at (A), you will see equal portions of the lines marked a and b, and they will have an equal slant. The same will be true of c and d. Now if you turn the cube so that it makes unequal angles with the line of sight as at (B), the line a will seem shorter and line b longer than before.

It is instructive at this stage to actually continue receding lines indefinitely, allowing them to meet at the proper points as at (C) and (D).

As a way to determine the correct drawing of a cube in angular perspective, it may help you to draw diagonal lines on a forshortened square as shown by the dotted lines in (A) and (B). At (A) with the cube turned at equal angles, the long diagonal is horizontal, the short perpendicular. If the cube is swung around as in (B), however, the diagonals immediately tip. Point g drops lower than e, and h moves to the right of f instead of remaining above it.

Figure 7. Study the cylinder in all sorts of positions above and below the eye. Such study and comparison will prove that the cylinder, regardless of position, always appears symmetrical about its long axis line and that the long diameters of the ellipses forming the ends will be at right angles to the axis of the cylinder.

You will also find that it is never possible to see quite halfway around the cylindrical surface. And when the farther end of the horizontal or tipped cylinder is a greater distance from the eye than the nearer end, it will appear smaller. This means in turn that the elements of the cylindrical surface will appear to converge, and these elements—being all parallel lines—will seem to vanish toward a point.

If the cylinder is placed horizontally, this point will be at eye level. If tipped in some other position, the point will be above or below the eye. To this same vanishing point, the axis of the cylinder, if drawn, will also recede. And you will also find that regardless of where the cylinder is placed those elements of the surface that form the straight boundaries will appear tangent to the curves of the bases.

In (A) the cylinder has been drawn within a square prism to show the relationship between objects based on the square and the circle.

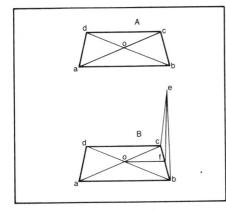

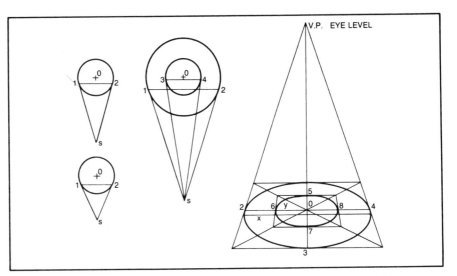

Figure 8. A square was drawn here with criss-crossing diagonals. This locates the true center of the square o as it appears in perspective. It seems more than halfway back because the farther half of the square, being a greater distance from the eye than the first half, seems smaller. For the same reason, line bo seems longer than od, though if viewed from the top they would be equal. This clarifies the fact that equal distances on any receding line seem unequal, the farther one seeming to be shorter.

Now suppose that at the end of this square a triangle is drawn as in (B). Locate its apex by drawing a line horizontally from the center o to line bc, erecting a vertical altitude at the point of intersection f, choosing point e arbitrarily on the altitude, and then drawing ec and eb. This triangle illustrates the truth that the apex of a vertical isosceles or equilateral triangle having a horizontal base appears in a vertical line erected in the perspective center of the base.

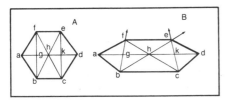

Figure 9. Study the perspective of a hexagon. Notice in (A) that the two short diagonals bf and ce and the long diagonals be and cf divide the long diagonal ad into four equal parts. When a hexagon is sketched in parallel perspective, as in (B), all sides appear equal.

Figure 10. Circles always appear in perspective as ellipses. The top view of a cylinder is drawn in (A). The viewer is standing at s. Lines of tangency from s to the cylinder give points at 1 and 2 that represent the extreme limits of the cylindrical surface visible from s. If you draw a straight line across the top of the cylinder from 1 to 2, it marks the greatest width of the cylinder as it appears from point s.

This line really does not pass through the true center of the circle, represented by o, but is between this center and the viewer and becomes the major axis of the ellipse representing the circle. The portion behind this line on the sketch appears from point s as exactly the same size as that portion left white. Hence the ellipse must appear truly symmetrical about this line. At (B) the viewer stands closer and so sees less of the cylindrical surface.

Suppose you have two concentric circles representing the tops of two concentric cylinders as indicated in (C), with the viewer still standing at s. If you treat these independently as before, drawing tangents to the curves, these tangents will measure off visible surfaces from 1 to 2 on the larger and from 3 to 4 on the smaller. This shows that the eye will see relatively more of the cylindrical surface of the smaller cylinder. Line 3–4 is nearer the center o than line 1–2,

but it does not pass through it.

The easiest way to draw such circles in perspective is to assume that they are inscribed in squares. In (D) two squares with a common center are shown in perspective. The crossing of the diagonals gives the true center of the circle at o, correctly located in perspective. The larger ellipse must pass through points 1, 2, 3, and 4. Line x, just halfway from points 1 and 3, is the long axis of the large ellipse, which is drawn symmetrically about this line, passing through points 1, 2, 3, and 4. The smaller ellipse is drawn exactly the same way passing through points 5, 6, 7, and 8 and drawn symmetrically about axis y, which is halfway from 5 to 7.

Study these circles in (D) and examine objects in which other concentric circles are found. Isn't it true that foreshortened concentric circles appear as ellipses? And shouldn't the short axis lines of these ellipses coincide? Notice too that distances 3–7, 7–o, o–5, and 5–1 on the short axis seem to decrease gradually, though actually at the same rate as the unforeshortened distances on the long axis, 2–6, 6–o, o–8, and 8–4. So in drawing such ellipses, remember to keep the space between them widest at the ends as at 2–6 and 8–4 and a little wider between the near curves at 3–7 than at the farther side 5–1.

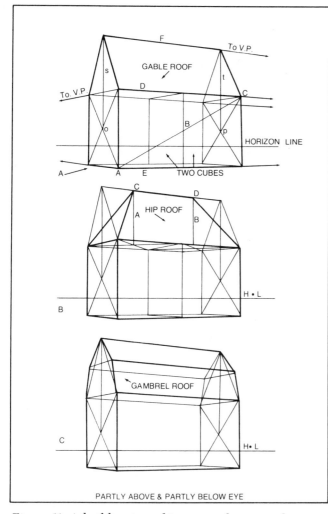

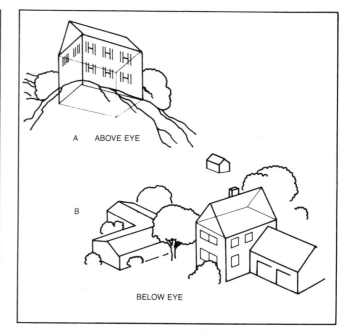

Figure 12. Apply the following geometric principles when drawing buildings above and below eye level: All horizontal lines and planes slope downward toward the horizon line as in (A) when above eye level or upward as in (B) when below eye level.

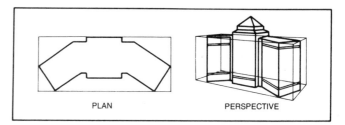

Figure 13. Complex structures should be reduced to their simplest geometric components. First draw the mass (shown with dashed lines) and then subdivide it into smaller parts.

Figure 11. A building is nothing more than a combination of simple geometric forms to which principles of perspective have been applied. For example, since the eye is usually from 4' to 5' (1 to 2 m) above ground, the horizon line is drawn in (A) a quarter of the way up the building. The nearest cube is worked over first until its proportion and perspective convergence seem satisfactory. Then lines D and E are produced indefinitely and a diagonal line AC carried through point B, exactly halfway from the ground to the eaves, automatically marking off the end of the second cube at C.

When the two cubes are completed, the roof is added. Centers o and p are located by drawing the diagonals of the square ends of the house. Vertical lines s and t are erected from these points, and these lines mark the height of the ridge F, which converges toward its correct vanishing point at the right. The sketch is the same in (B), except that the roof is hipped instead of gabled. The ends of the ridge are located by erecting perpendicular lines A and B through the intersection points of the diagonals of the tops of the two cubes forming the house. The sketch in (C) shows a gambrel roof, with a gable drawn first as a guide as shown in (A).

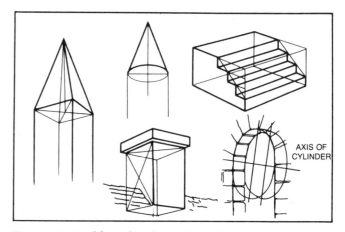

Figure 14. Building details, such as the towers, chimney, steps, and archway shown here, are also based on the same basic principles of perspective.

suring distances, and other shortcuts, which will help you save time and sketch accurately.

Sometimes you may want to draw buildings entirely above the eye, as on a high hill or mountain, or below the eye. Figure 12 gives simple examples of each type of perspective.

By now you should know that whether buildings are above or below the eye or at its level, whether simple or complex, the same general principles hold true. But when a building is complicated in its masses or irregular in plan, it is best to think of it as enclosed within a simpler mass and draw that first, subdividing it into smaller parts later. In Figure 13 the lighter lines show the simple mass that was drawn first.

After the larger proportions of a building are established, many details must be added. Figure 14 shows a few typical ones drawn in a basic style. Many towers are based on pyramids and cones, such as those shown in (A) and (B). Practice these, and then try your hand at steps, chimneys, arches, dormers, and so forth until you feel able to sketch any of the more common details easily and well, either from the objects themselves (which is excellent practice) or from memory.

Figure 15 shows that it is also best to block the mass in very simply when drawing furniture. To perfect your skill, cut out prints of buildings and pieces of furniture and sketch simple shapes around them with a few lines, preferably straight. This will help you see that all objects are comparatively simple in basic form.

Photographs or prints can help you study perspective in another way. For example, lay a ruler, T-square, or triangle on them and draw with a pencil the various series of parallel lines moving toward their vanishing points, locating and drawing the eye level or horizon line first. This will help you understand the phenomenon of perspective more quickly than perhaps any other exercise.

See Chapter 9 for a comprehensive discussion of drawing from photographs.

INTERIORS

Interiors are drawn in just the same way as exteriors, only you are looking at the inside of the cubes and prisms

rather than the outside. This means that in order to draw interiors you simply remove those exteriors nearest to you. Rooms themselves are usually very simple in form. It's the furniture, turned at various angles and of irregular shapes, that may give you the greatest difficulty. A little practice, however, will make you proficient in this type of drawing.

See Chapter 7 for further discussion of interiors, including furniture.

A FEW MORE HINTS

Regardless of your subject, always look constantly in the same fixed direction until you finish the drawing. Although in practice this isn't very hard to do when an object is small, large objects or entire rooms or buildings require you to study details one at a time. Therefore it's easy to make a composite sketch in which the various small parts may be correct in themselves, but wrong when considered in relation to one another and to the whole. When drawing a room, for instance, it's easy to go astray by looking first at a window and drawing that and then doing a door and so on, one thing at a time.

With this method the whole is sure to look distorted. For this reason, locate a horizon line on the drawing whenever possible and find vanishing points if these come naturally within the paper area. In sketching the main lines, try to give them the right proportion and perspective convergence. If you build up a correct framework for the whole, it won't be hard to add the detail. Therefore spend plenty of time on this preliminary work. If you find it too difficult to draw from actual buildings, sketch from photographs for a while, since this is much easier to do. Then go on to portions of interiors and exteriors before attempting the whole.

The drawing by Ernest Watson in Figure 16 shows the type of subject that is extremely difficult to block out because of the great number of converging lines unless you are familiar with the principles of perspective involved. A word of warning: If a subject like this is not constructed correctly, the errors will be glaringly apparent, regardless of the quality of the technique.

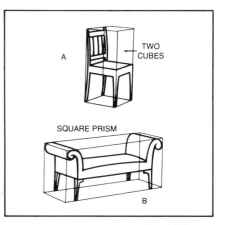

Figure 15. Furniture too should be reduced to its simplest geometric forms. For the chair in (A) two cubes were drawn in dotted lines, while the seat in (B) was sketched within a square prism. When objects are enclosed within simple forms (think of it as being "frozen in a block of ice"), you are less likely to draw them incorrectly in perspective.

Pennsylvania Station
from Grant Boulevard
PITTSBURG
Ernest W. Watson
June 1911

Figure 16. Note all the principles of perspective involved in this drawing by Ernest W. Watson.

PART TWO

CAPTURING BUILDINGS, INTERIORS, AND SURROUNDINGS:
TECHNIQUES AND EXAMPLES

The first five chapters set out important practical techniques for creating visual effects through pencil and ink. The next several chapters offer you imaginative, proven methods for translating this knowledge into sketching and rendering actual buildings, their interiors and furnishings, as well as the surroundings such as trees, sky, clouds, and water that, in every drawing, are vital complements to the buildings themselves.

When drawing architecture, keep in mind several key pointers. Compose each drawing with care, building it up from outline to detail. Establish carefully the key elements, determining the foreground, middleground, and background so as to obtain a sense of depth and scale. Scrupulously select the effect or mood you want to create and select your medium accordingly. Pay special attention to including detail in your building, because only that way will you capture its essential texture. Perhaps above all, plan how to use light, shade, and shadow, as these will determine the modeling, focus, mood, and excitement of your drawing.

Each of the three chapters that demonstrate techniques for capturing a building and its interiors or landscape is followed by a rich selection of drawings covering many periods and styles. By examining how great artists and designers have depicted architecture in ink and pencil, you will gain inspiration from the great range of sketching and rendering possibilities that can be created from those two humble media.

This part concludes with a chapter on drawing from photographs, which is a useful technique to know, either when you're just beginning or when dictated by circumstances.

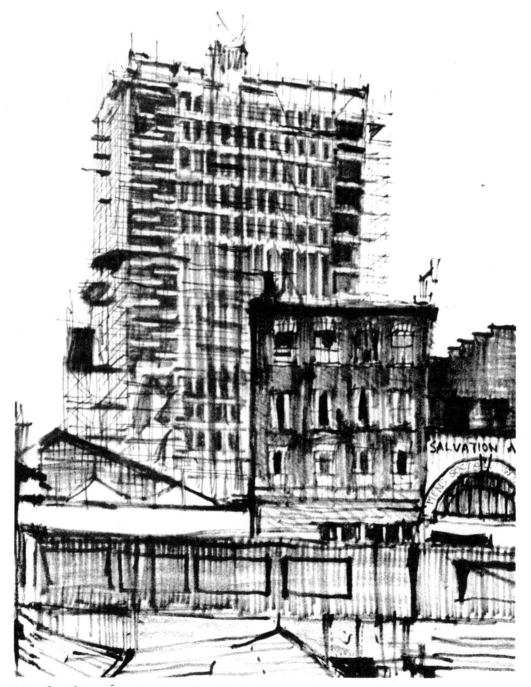

Note that this composition is really a detail of the complete work shown on page 45, although it is able to stand on its own unlike other details shown elsewhere in this chapter.

CHAPTER SIX
BUILDINGS

Before you select a particular building or a group of buildings to draw, there are a few points about composition and technique that will help you create dynamic work. How depth and dimension, detail and texture, sunlight and shadow can be useful in drawing or rendering architectural subjects are also discussed in this chapter.

BUILDING A DRAWING

Building a drawing is a matter of balance: One area of weight has to be balanced by another. This is all part of selecting your subject matter and should be considered carefully when choosing your vantage point.

The building process is called "composition." It is the arrangement of all the various elements inside the intended shape and size of the drawing. In drawing still-life subjects the problem is easy: You just arrange objects to your liking. But to arrange buildings to your liking often requires a great deal of study and evaluation. Make a rule about this: Instead of beginning work on the first view that pleases you, search for two or three alternate vantage point before deciding from which to make your drawing.

Always, before you draw a line, think hard about what you see. Even the most complex subjects can be reduced to simple terms. Look at the drawing shown on page 42. While this may seem to be a complex subject, it has been reduced to simple terms in the pencil drawing at the top of the page. As an exercise, try reducing similar scenes to a few main construction lines like this. Do them quite small, no bigger than the one above.

After you experiment with a variety of compositions (an example is shown on page 43), balance will become instinctive. Cutting a window out of a piece of cardboard, as shown in the example, and looking through it with one eye closed will help you arrange a composition, or you can use your hands as shown in the accompanying drawing.

TECHNIQUE

"Technique" can be described as a means of using a medium or media together to produce a certain style or effect. The use of pen and wash, for instance, is a technique.

By technique you should not produce a collection of clichés or tricks for drawing certain objects. Too many people have developed their style of drawing in this manner; they have a set way of doing a glass office tower or of rendering trees in the distance or even of adding texture in the foreground. How uninspiring it is to see a collection of such drawings. This is not true drawing, but a means of making a pretty picture, which has no depth or feeling.

You must realize as early as possible that you should draw *what you see*, not what you think you see. This is all that true drawing really is: training yourself to see accurately and then putting down on paper, without any false representation, what you have seen. A good test, if you suspect you may be falling into this trap, is to place three or four drawings together to see if there is any particular object among them that is drawn identically.

There are no set rules about which medium to use. If you feel you can make a better drawing by using shoe polish and a brush, go ahead and do

so. Don't limit yourself to only one or two media; experiment with them all. Only by having a wide range of techniques at your command can you select the one most suitable for a particular drawing.

You may find a rough surfaced paper and soft black pencil or thin brush an exciting method of working. You may find that the felt-tipped pen is useful for quick sketching and for catching the atmosphere of a building. There are examples of many very different techniques in this book.

"Style" is a word often confused with technique. What does it mean, and how is it that one artist has developed a manner or style that distinguishes his or her drawings from all others?

A sincere individual style cannot be taught. It can only develop naturally and slowly. It cannot be forced, because it should spring from the quality of mind *behind* the drawing. So don't worry about it at this stage. Keep working and it will come to you as your interest in drawing develops, as your knowledge of your subject matter increases, and as your hand becomes more practiced.

DEPTH AND DIMENSION

Getting "depth" into your drawing will seem difficult at first. While correct perspective—such as the way buildings and roads vanish away from you—is important, depth can also be increased by varying the weight of line in a drawing. The basic rule to apply is this: the nearer the object, the heavier you should draw it.

The following exercise, which you can carry out at home, will help you understand and solve this problem. Set up a still-life composition of, say,

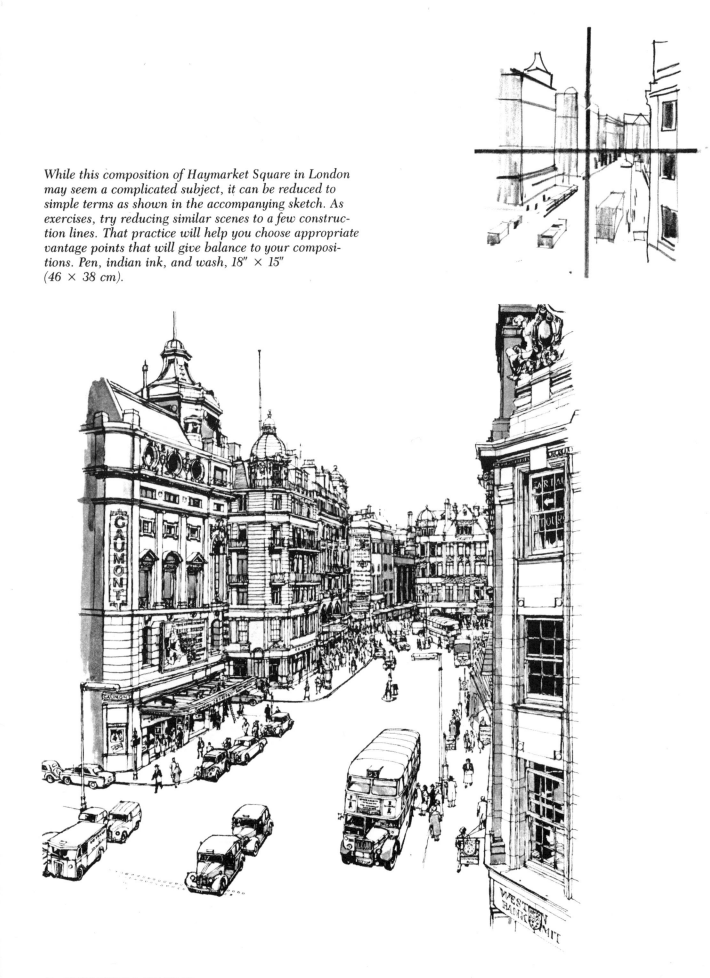

While this composition of Haymarket Square in London may seem a complicated subject, it can be reduced to simple terms as shown in the accompanying sketch. As exercises, try reducing similar scenes to a few construction lines. That practice will help you choose appropriate vantage points that will give balance to your compositions. Pen, indian ink, and wash, 18" × 15" (46 × 38 cm).

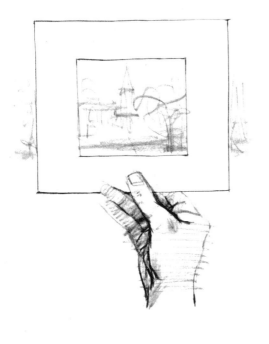

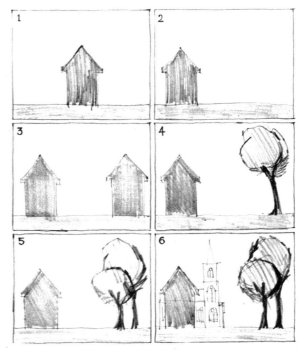

The first diagram is an example of balance in its simplest form: the house is central and the white spaces on each side are equal. Note from this that a tall building should always be placed slightly off center. The second diagram, however, is too one-sided. Some weight is added in 3. Balance is now perfect; in fact, diagrams 1 and 3 are equal.

However, the composition is boring, so let's add a tree. Balance is maintained and interest increased. A second tree in 5 adds further interest. If a church is added as in 6, not only are balance and interest maintained, but the composition now has a focal point.

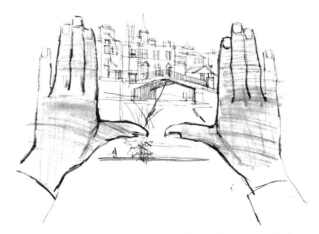

Here are two sketches of drawings that appear later in this chapter. In the top one the projecting railing on the right balances the building on the left (as related to 3 above). In the other drawing the dark tree adds interest and balance as in 4. Place your finger over the railing or tree to see how the balance can be upset, as well as what is needed to achieve balance.

To arrange a composition, use your hands as shown in the drawing or cut a window out of a piece of cardboard (shown above) and look through it with one eye closed.

The composition here presents no problem: the house is central. Concentrate first on tone and shape, considering them as one. Build up the main construction lines and masses of tone very simply and broadly, first getting the shape correct in perspective and proportion.

(1)

(2)

(3)

When looking at groups of buildings (1), half close your eyes so that you see no details at all—only shapes (2) or areas of tone. The outlines of these shapes are the main construction lines (3). These are the first lines to draw.

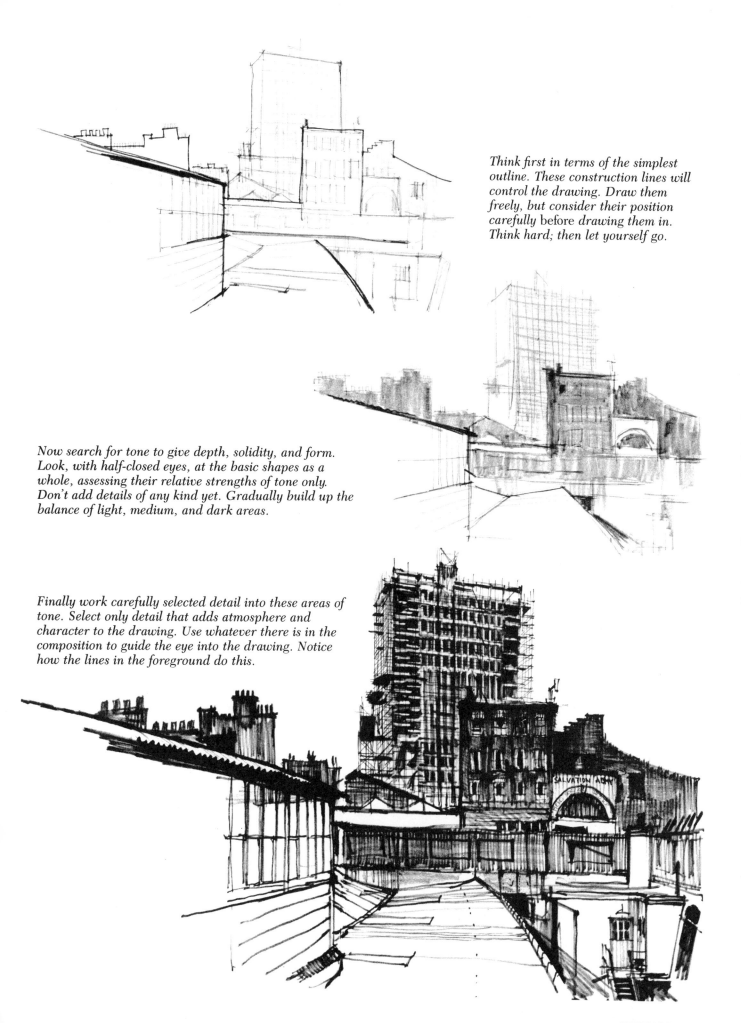

Think first in terms of the simplest outline. These construction lines will control the drawing. Draw them freely, but consider their position carefully before drawing them in. Think hard; then let yourself go.

Now search for tone to give depth, solidity, and form. Look, with half-closed eyes, at the basic shapes as a whole, assessing their relative strengths of tone only. Don't add details of any kind yet. Gradually build up the balance of light, medium, and dark areas.

Finally work carefully selected detail into these areas of tone. Select only detail that adds atmosphere and character to the drawing. Use whatever there is in the composition to guide the eye into the drawing. Notice how the lines in the foreground do this.

a jug, a glass, and a pot or two. Make an interesting grouping of them. Now draw them as a whole, remembering that you are going to draw whatever is nearest you in a *stronger line*. The object farthest away should be drawn more lightly.

At the same time try to *feel* your way around the objects as you draw. Try to feel the space between the front of the jug and the back of it, even if you cannot see the back. If you apply what you learn from this exercise to drawing buildings you will give the buildings greater solidity; you will show how the walls recede; you will give your drawing depth. If you are making a pen drawing or shading with pencil, for instance, the sensitive use of graduated tone will also help convey depth.

Whatever the subject you are drawing, it is made up of a foreground, a middle distance, and a background. It is the middle distance that is so often the most difficult to draw, especially if the subject is a landscape without objects in the composition. Objects are needed to give a sense of proportion. The most helpful of all are things you know the size of already, like the traffic in the drawing on page 42.

DETAIL AND TEXTURE

Attention to detail and texture is a great help in composing a drawing. It can give added interest to the composition and help the viewer's eye move easily around the picture.

"Texture" can be defined as the pattern made by the various materials in an object. A row of windows on a large building, for example, will give texture. Detail is not quite the same thing, although the two together certainly give a pattern.

When walking in a city or neighborhood or when traveling in a car or bus, look for different textures. Notice the different effects of texture given by the varied materials used in buildings—brick, stone, wood, adobe, tile, concrete, glass, steel. Notice pattern too and imagine how you would indicate these differences in your sketches.

In the drawing made with a fountain pen on the bottom of page 49, see what compelled the artist to draw it. Look at the varying texture and pattern in the buildings. Look at the brickwork. Notice that the tall build-

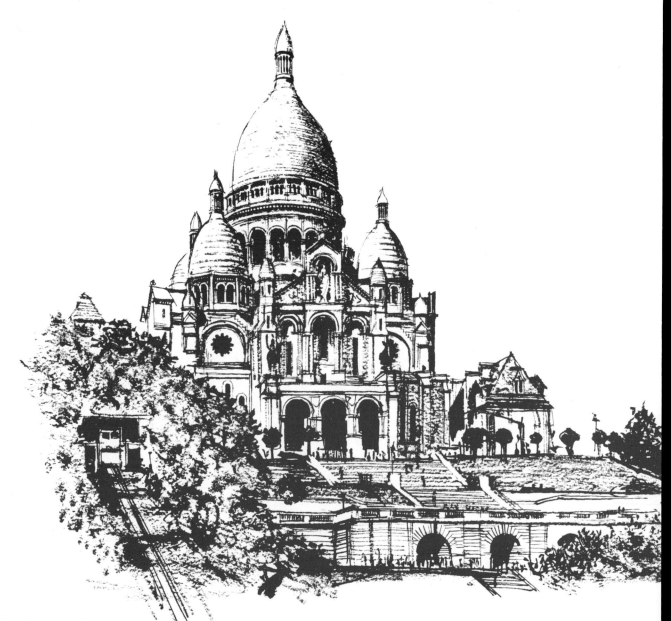

In this drawing a variety of different materials have been used to give it atmosphere: wash, body color, pen and indian ink, fountain pen, and pastel. There are no set rules about what to use; use anything you like.

This drawing of Sacré Coeur in Paris is an example of what is known as "dry brush" technique. Use a fairly rough paper for this and either indian ink (with no water) or black poster paint. Make sure you don't have too much paint or ink on the brush; then "drag" it across the surface of the paper. This will give you a medium tone into which you can work. Also try using a dark paper, even black if you like, with white poster paint. A very satisfying effect can be achieved this way. 8½" × 20" (22 × 51 cm).

This is a free and rapidly sketched drawing of a street corner in Paris, done in fountain pen and blue ink on smooth white bond paper. 10″ × 9″ (25 × 23 cm).

This drawing was made entirely with a felt-tip pen on smooth white bond paper. Felt tips are extremely useful for broad, simple treatments needed to emphasize size and mass in buildings. 12″ × 14″ (31 × 36 cm).

Depth can be created by varying the weight of line used in a drawing. Note how the rule—the nearer the object the heavier you should draw it—has been applied here. Objects are also needed to give a sense of dimension. The most helpful are those you already know the size of—like the tree and fence shown here.

Composition can be imposed on a drawing, however complex, by simplification, by the subtle emphasis of main construction lines, and by the elimination of detail in carefully selected areas. Here the area on the sides has been left bare and texture confined to the center, a common treatment. Notice how these areas of texture draw the eye to the center of the drawing.

Chisel (or flat leaded) pencils, with which this drawing was made, are useful for putting in large areas of tone. They can be combined particularly well with a felt-tip pen for quick impressions and for working out composition. Sharpen the lead as you would a chisel and use the pencil like a flat brush.

ing to the left has been deliberately kept free of brickwork. Why? Because, had it been added, the drawing would have become monotonous.

The reasons for this need to be explained more clearly. They are most important for you to grasp. When you draw a subject you are recording what you see and putting it down on paper. But you do not want to record it *identically*; the camera does that. You can do more. You can *select* from the subject things that interest you and leave out what is unnecessary or what confuses your design. You want the viewer's eye to wander around the drawing at random, enjoying everything he or she sees. Composition goes far in achieving this; detail and texture, used intelligently, do the rest.

Take another look at the drawing referred to above. Notice how the detail varies from one area to another. You might say to yourself: "Well, the brickwork was there to be drawn."

Yes, but there was also patterning on all the other buildings. Can you see now that the area left undrawn is terribly important? It acts as a resting place for the eye before it goes off in another direction. It also helps keep the composition from becoming too monotonous in detail and texture.

You must also learn to be selective in this way.

Looking at the drawing as a whole you may well say to yourself, "I haven't got the patience to do all that detail." If you persevere, however, you will find drawing very rewarding and satisfying.

SUNLIGHT AND SHADOW

Shadows cast by buildings in direct sunlight can produce interesting effects. The drawing here is a study in shade with very little line work at all; the sun, in fact, was almost opposite where the artist worked.

The drawing shows how tone can give depth to a drawing and pull it

together as a whole. From the start the shadow is the most important element in the composition. When drawing a subject such as this, try putting in the shadow first. Use a chisel pencil quite loosely; don't worry if you don't get the exact shape of the shadowed area; allow yourself freedom. By doing it this way the result will be more spontaneous. Then start working into the drawing with a sharp-pointed pencil; search the form for detail and texture.

It is important to differentiate between tone and shadow. They are not the same thing. Shadows in a drawing can be in different tones, darker or lighter, and so can colors.

Early evening shadows can be very useful in a drawing. If you find it difficult to get the shadows in before the sun disappears, you can complete your drawing earlier in the day and at the appropriate time go back and quickly put in the shadows with a chisel pencil or brush and wash.

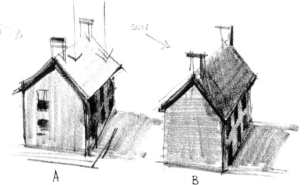

The difference between tone and shadow is illustrated on the right. Suppose for a minute that the roof and the walls of a house are exactly the same color. Now the light from the sky would make the roof lighter in tone *than the walls*; house (A) shows this. However, roof tiles are usually darker in color and tone than the brickwork or stone of the walls. House (B) has the darker roof because the color, *not the tone*, has been added. In fact you have to decide carefully before you start a picture which is color and which is tone.

Note examples above and below that show how shadows can be the most important, interesting elements in your drawings.

EXAMPLES

The drawings of buildings on the following pages give you a practical insight into the imaginative kinds of sketching and rendering that can be achieved using the two media of pencil and ink. They include the work of a wide range of artists and designers. Study them for the way they relate the building to the overall drawing, how they portray roof lines, scale, windows, doors, and other openings, how they capture different materials and finishes, unusual details, and the various other elements that make up a drawing's mood.

The three elevations of Julia Morgan's Bell Tower for Mills College in Oakland, California, dated August 1903, show the architect's traditional technique of beginning a design by making studies, in this case in graphite pencil on medium- to heavyweight rag tracing paper using a T-square, straightedge, and triangle. A rational, practical designer, who was the first woman to graduate from the École des Beaux-Arts in Paris, she built the tower in reinforced concrete, but clothed it in an historic style, in this case Mission Revival, with tiled roof and round arches. That the tower withstood the 1906 San Francisco earthquake led to commissions, including the reconstruction of the Fairmont Hotel. This drawing, 37¾" × 24½" (96 × 62 cm), is one of the few by Morgan that remain, since she destroyed many when she closed her office in 1952.

Courtesy Documents Collection, College of Environmental Design, University of California, Berkeley.

A TRADITIONAL APPROACH TO DRAWING: JULIA MORGAN

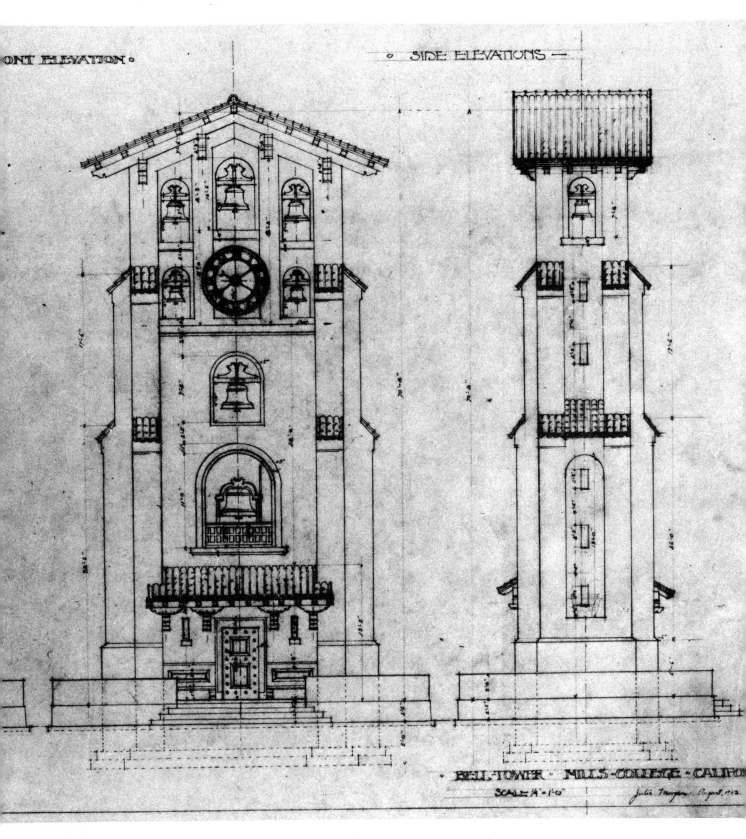

ONT ELEVATION ·

· SIDE ELEVATIONS —

· BELL·TOWER· MILLS·COLLEGE· CALIFO

SCALE 1/4" = 1'-0"

EVOKING ATMOSPHERE: TURNER BROOKS

Evoking an atmospheric vision of a building is Turner Brooks' intention in his drawings. This aerial perspective for the Provincetown Playhouse and Eugene O'Neill Archival Center in Provincetown, Massachusetts, became an image of a ship steaming through the night, with lights reflecting off the water and mist. While Brooks admits that there is much more to designing than this, "it is image more than anything else that takes possession of me and drives me through the design process." This drawing, done in charcoal on paper 36″ × 40″ (86 × 102 cm), made the project more real for Brooks than any line drawing or model could.

PORTRAYING CHARACTER: JAMES COOTE

Images that suggest atmosphere and character appeal more to James Coote than those that describe geometry or intellectual order. This approach to the Browder House in Austin, Texas, is one such example. Drawn freehand in 1981 in pencil on heavy white tracing paper (Albanene) this perspective is 23″ × 34″ (58 × 86 cm). Although he uses many kinds of views, Coote relies heavily on perspectives, which he finds useful to show abstract concepts, often basing his drawings on slides of the site. Coote draws both sketches and presentation drawings in graphite because he likes the medium's suggestive and responsive qualities.

DRAWING FOR REPRODUCTION: RAYMOND HOOD AND ELIEL SAARINEN

In the 1920s pencil on vellum largely replaced ink on waxed linen as a presentation technique in design offices because new reproduction methods produced excellent copies from the vellum, and few offices could afford to pay draftsmen to make working drawings in ink. The Chicago Tribune Tower competition of 1922 therefore produced a whole array of fine drawings using pencil on vellum.

The winning design by Raymond Hood, of the firm Howells and Hood (right), is a fine example of how presentation drawings were used to convey architectural intent. Plans, elevations, and sections were required of competitors, but the outside perspective was paramount. This drawing captures the great vertical sweep of the neo-Gothic design, using thin lines and light shading.

Eliel Saarinen won second prize. His design (opposite page) employs an even finer line, thereby adding a somewhat unreal quality to the proposed tower.

Courtesy Tribune Tower Competition, The Tribune Company, 1923.

EXPRESSING THE ROMANTIC ESSENCE OF THE SKYSCRAPER: CESAR PELLI

Cesar Pelli evokes the spirit of Hugh Ferriss (see pages 178–187 for a look at Ferriss's work) in these perspective drawings for a corporate headquarters building in Pittsburgh, Pennsylvania. The diagonal lines, drawn with a stabilo pencil on vellum, have become a style for which Pelli's office is known and that Pelli feels is "a particularly appropriate representation of my own architecture." Used to express surface, light, shadow, and volume, each line is layered one upon another to build density and to control value. Many of the chance visual qualities of architecture, like reflections and transparency, can also be suggested by this technique. Pelli first learned the technique in the office of Eero Saarinen, and it is the same one Eliel Saarinen used for the Chicago Tribune Competition in 1922 (see page 59). The drawing here is 24″ × 16″ (61 × 41 cm), and the one on the facing page is 6″ × 3″ (15 × 8 cm).

INTEGRATING OLD AND NEW: HENRY MELTZER AND RICHARD OLIVER

The intent of these elevation drawings for the Dewey House in Santa Fe, New Mexico, was to show that in form and detail the new additions were sympathetic to the style of the original parts. Pencil was used because it could render both soft, massive volumes of the additions and original parts, as well as the crisp wood trim and detail around the doors, windows, and portals of the enlarged house. Prismacolor pencils were used on yellow tracing paper, with an underlay of pencil to show the major architectural lines. The drawings are 16″ × 32″ (41 × 81 cm). The soft, pictorial technique was inspired by the drawings of Michael Graves.

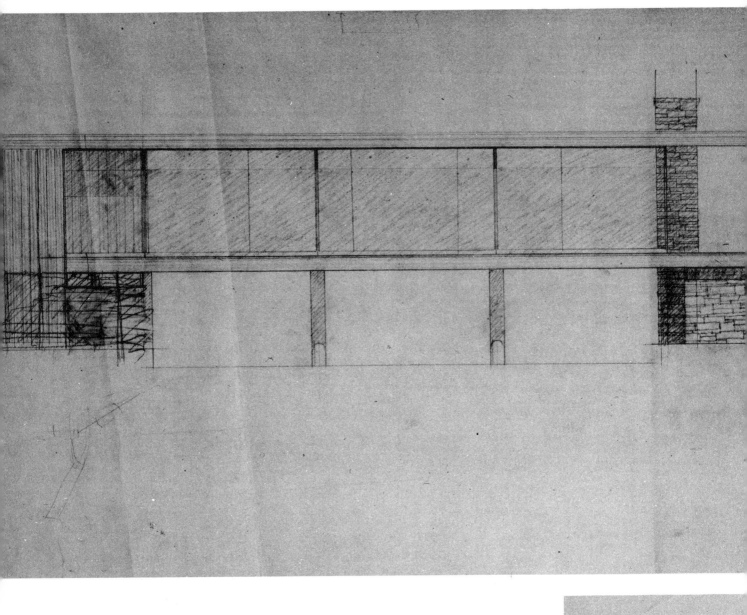

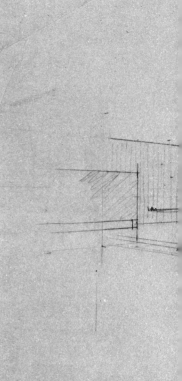

DELINEATING "SKIN AND BONES" ARCHITECTURE: MIES VAN DER ROHE

Ludwig Mies van der Rohe used pencil and yellow crayon pencil on tracing paper to capture the outline and subtle proportions of this Jackson Hole, Wyoming, house for the Resor family, his first United States client. Sharply pointed pencils also create delicate flat tones for windows, the second floor siding, the stone-faced wall on the fifth bay from the left, and the adjacent chimney (above), as well as the columns and partitions of the living room (right). Mies labeled the understated quality of his building enclosures "skin and bones" architecture, and pencil served him well as he sought to express it in his drawings. The north elevation of the Resor house project (above) is 20″ × 42″ (51 × 107 cm); the living room (right) is 12″ × 18″ (31 × 46 cm).

Courtesy Mies van der Rohe Archive, The Museum of Modern Art, New York, New York.

A VERSATILE LINE TECHNIQUE: GERALD ALLEN

The 1980 perspective and choisy-metric drawings of a
rustic shelter for New York's Central Park are examples of
a quick and quite easy technique that Gerald Allen
began to use that year. The drawings were roughly laid
out about three to four feet wide in pencil, with the final
inked with a felt-tip pen. Then they were reduced
photographically to film negatives 12″ × 12″ (30 × 30
cm), and contact prints were made from these on
translucent Mylar, which became the "originals." Suited
to meet many needs, they reproduce well over and over
again. Although the lines are thin, they survive crude
reproduction processes and further reductions because
they are all about the same weight and can therefore be
uniformly overexposed by a copy camera. The thin black
lines floating on pearly white backgrounds also seem to
please Allen's clients.

The delineator was Michael Barclay.

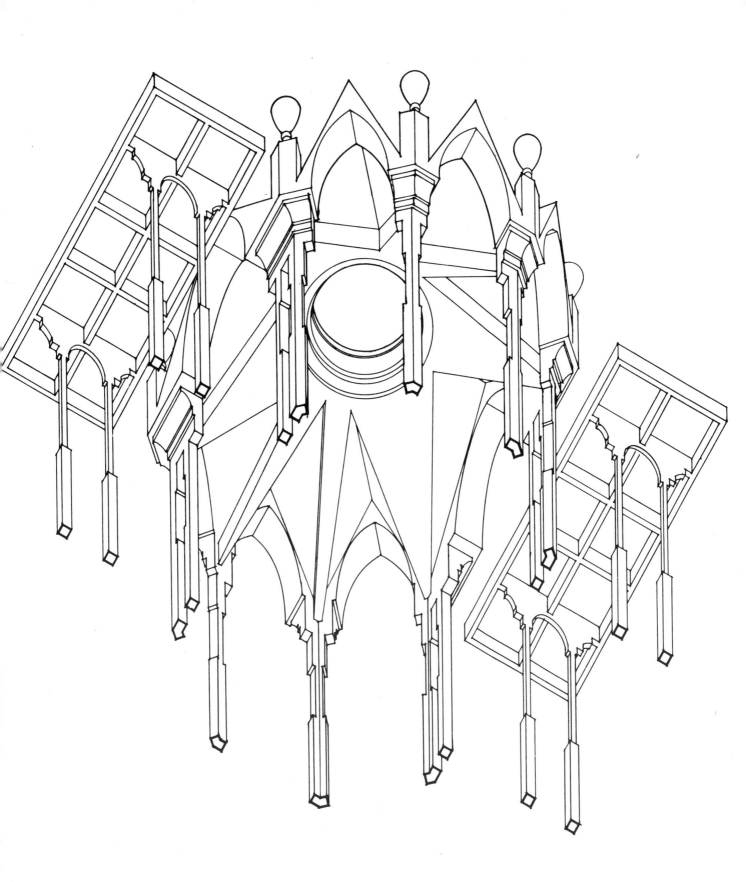

CREATING RHYTHM FROM LINE: EERO SAARINEN

The great versatility of pencil is shown in these two studies of Eero Saarinen's Ingalls Rink at Yale University. Both studies were done in dark pencil on 8½″ × 11″ (22 × 28 cm) yellow notebook paper. In the plan study the soft pencil captures the sensuous curves of the building's contour and the adjacent parking. The perspective study likewise shows how pencil was able to evoke the rhythm of the great concrete spine from which the cable roof over the rink is hung.

Courtesy Eero Saarinen Papers, Yale University Library, New Haven, Connecticut.

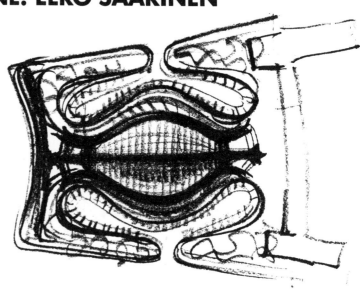

EVOKING MONUMENTALITY
BY SIMPLE MEANS: WHITNEY WARREN

Black ink and pencil on tracing paper were used by
architect Whitney Warren to evoke, in this original
sketch, the majestic south facade of Grand Central
Terminal in New York. Despite its simple line work,
this small, 4½″ × 11″ (11 × 28 cm) sketch, done in
1910, captures in swift, easy pen strokes and rapid
pencil shading of window areas the main proportions
and chief elements of this monument: the great
arched windows and the pitched roof with its heavy
baroque sculpture.

Courtesy Cooper-Hewitt Museum, The Smith-
sonian Institution's National Museum of Design.
Gift of Mrs. William Greenough, 1943-51-13.

The original sketch for the facade
of the Grand Central Terminal New[?]
Whitney Warren
1910

POWER THROUGH THE CONCEPTUAL SKETCH: HENRY HOBSON RICHARDSON

One aspect of Henry Hobson Richardson's legacy is that he freed American architecture from European domination. Educated at the École des Beaux-Arts in Paris, Richardson began every design with a conceptual sketch, indicating in plan both the layout of the rooms and a sense of the superstructure. The plan for the Young Men's Association Library Competition of 1884 in Buffalo New York (opposite page), drawn 17¾" × 11¾" (45 × 30 cm) in India ink and pencil on stiff white paper, shows a continuity of spaces so characteristic of his work. In the 12" × 19¾" (31 × 50 cm) study in brown ink over pencil for an unidentified church reproduced here from a sketchbook dated 1869–1876, Richardson reveals that he thought of the elevation, as he did the plan, as a composition of large basic forms. It is the outline of the large mass, rather than the detail of the Romanesque Revival building, that conveys the drawing's power.

Courtesy Houghton Library, Harvard University, Cambridge, Massachusetts.

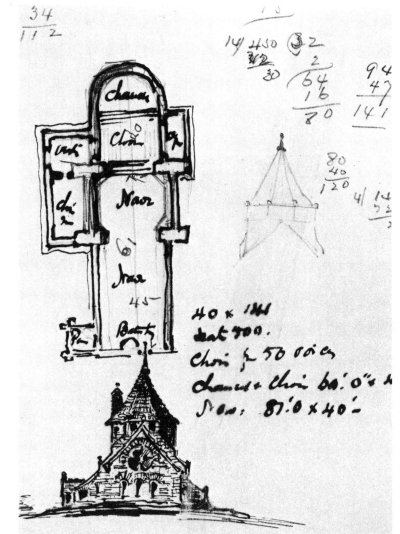

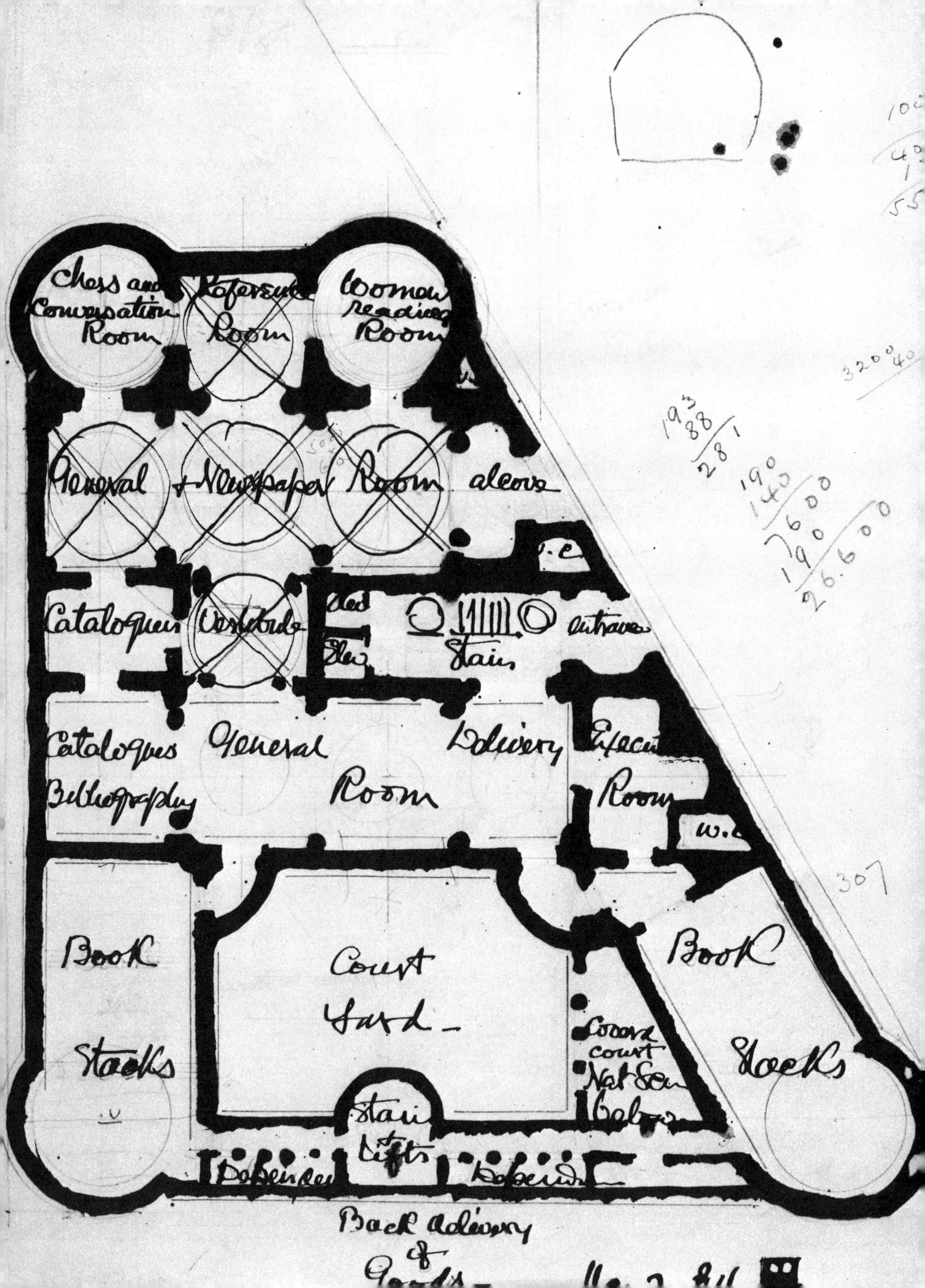

Chess and Conversation Room

Reference Room

Woman's reading Room

General + Newspaper Room   alcove

Catalogues   Vestibule   Cloak   stairs   entrance

Catalogues   General   Delivery   Execut

Bibliography   Room   Room   w.c

Book   Book

Court Yard

Stacks   Coons court   Stacks
Nat Son
Below

Stair
Lifts

Defender   Defender

Back delivery
of
Goods

ELEVATION : ON : BROAD : STREET :

PORTRAYING A RICH VARIETY OF MATERIALS: FRANK FURNESS

Frank Furness's work is admired today for its aggressive forms and unusual scale, as well as its freewheeling spirit. He fused the ideas of the leading theoreticians of the day: John Ruskin who advocated decoration as the essential ingredient of beautiful work and Viollet-le-Duc who believed that architecture should be derived from structure. This 1873 ink and wash elevation, 25½″ × 34½″ (65 × 88 cm), of the Pennsylvania Academy of the Fine Arts in Philadelphia shows how Furness combined both Italian and French architecture in the academy's facade. Constructed of a rich variety of materials, it is the unusual scale contrasts and the distinctive ornamentation that make the building so original.

Courtesy Pennsylvania Academy of the Fine Arts, Philadelphia, Pennsylvania.

DRY BRUSH CREATES DRAMA: SAMUEL CHAMBERLAIN

In this technique the brush is only partially dry and the paper is rough, so each brush stroke is broken in an interesting way. In this dry brush drawing, which he called Abbeville, Samuel Chamberlain combines ink lines and tones of great variety, both in size and character.

INTERPRETING MATERIALS:
BERTRAM GROSVENOR GOODHUE

In this pen and ink rendering of the completed chapel from the cloister of St. Thomas' College in Washington, D.C., Bertram Grosvenor Goodhue displays his mastery of drawing stonework, brickwork, clouds, and grass. Note the different ways in which crosshatch has been employed. The architects were Cram, Goodhue, and Ferguson.

DRAWING IN STAGES: VENTURI RAUCH SCOTT-BROWN

This 21½″ × 28″ (55 × 71 cm) drawing was done in
stages. First an ink base was laid down. This was
photographed by the KC5 process, areas of pantone were
applied, and the resulting image was rephotographed.
The 1975 drawing captures both the hilly site of this Vail
Village, Colorado, house, known as the Brant-Johnson
house, as well as the hint of European vernacular
wooden architecture.

 Courtesy Collection of Venturi Rauch Scott-Brown,
Philadelphia, Pennsylvania.

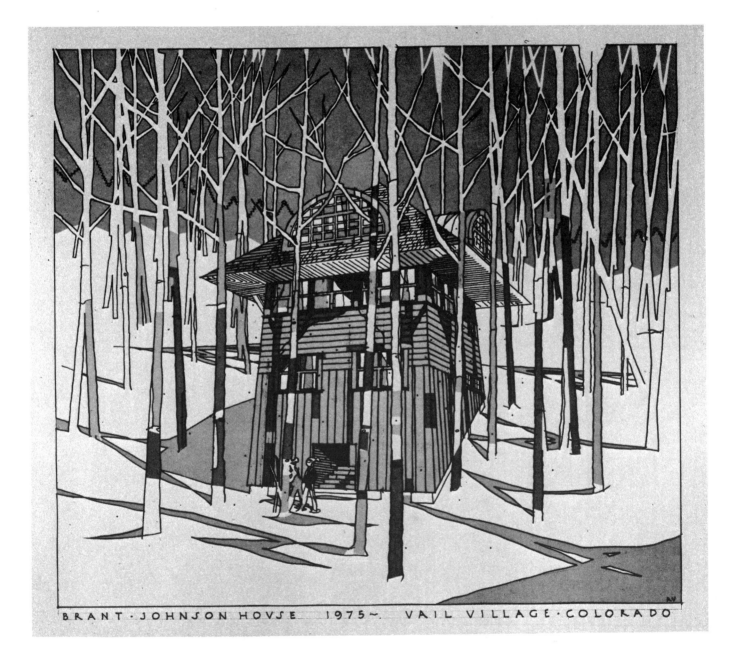

BRANT·JOHNSON HOVSE 1975~ VAIL VILLAGE·COLORADO

EXPLORING CHARACTER THROUGH SKETCHES: MICHAEL GRAVES

The sketches on these three pages were done in black ink on vellum using a Rapidograph pen. Michael Graves recomposed these drawings from his sketchbooks to fit on 8½″ × 11″ (22 × 28 cm) paper. His intent was to show the city of Portland, Oregon, as part of the final competition submission for the Portland Public Office Building, the creation and development of the building's form. He included the sheets of drawings with a booklet illustrating the scheme. For Graves, such drawings and studies, with which he fill his sketchbooks, represent a visual diary—a means of recording, remembering, and developing architectural ideas.

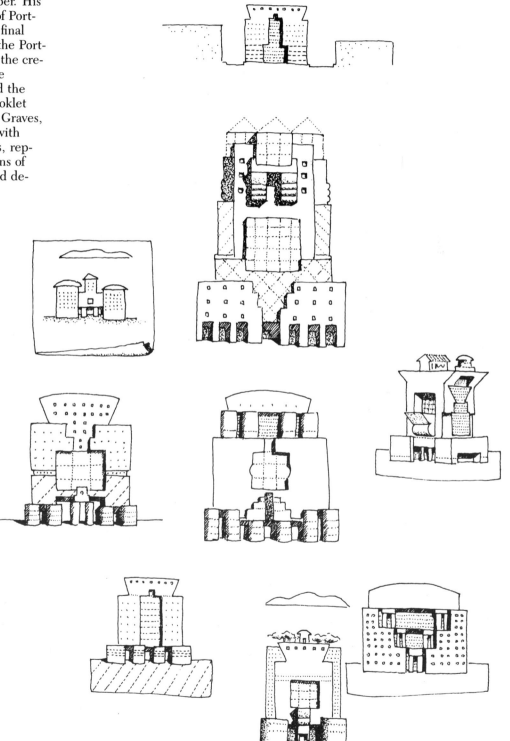

facade studies · Portland
graves

MICHAEL GRAVES

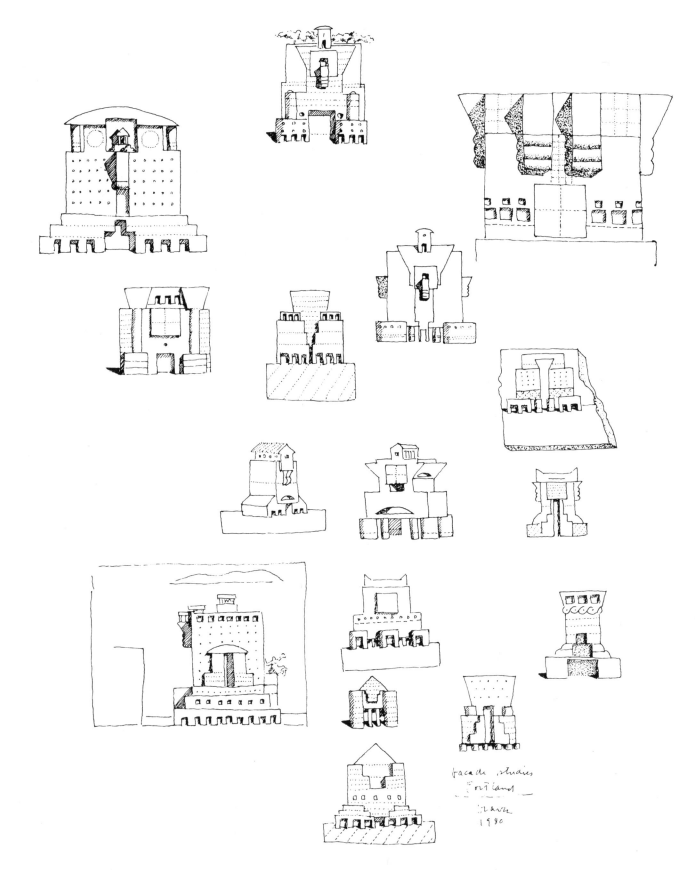

facade studies
Portland
Graves
1980

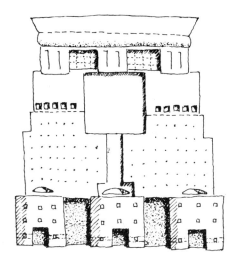

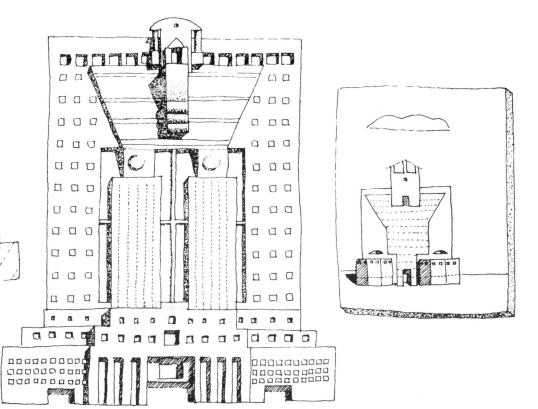

facade studies. Portland
Graves
'80

RENDERING DETAIL AND TEXTURE: ARTHUR GUPTILL

Cornices project from walls, and the drawing must suggest this projection. This is done in part by correctly delineating the form in outline, in part through application of light and shade. The most natural way to do this is to leave the projecting part light in value, in contrast with the tone denoting shade and shadow. The size of shadow suggests the amount of overhang. In this drawing the shadows also manage to express the various materials.

INDICATING BRICK AND STONEWORK: ARTHUR GUPTILL

Different types of brickwork are shown on sketches
1 through 3, brick and tile on sketch 4, and stone or slate
on sketches 5 through 7, with thatch also indicated on 6.
Do not attempt to show every brick course or each stone,
but the materials shown should leave no doubt as to what
they are.

SIMPLIFYING DETAIL: ERNEST PEIXOTTO

In this pen and ink drawing of a fountain at the Palazzo
Podestor in Genoa, Italy, the artist cleverly suggests the
balusters above and the iron rail below. Note the variety
of treatment of the balusters. The foliage too is rendered
with great freedom.

CAPTURING DEPTH WITHOUT USING PERSPECTIVE: SCHELL LEWIS

This drawing by the celebrated renderer Schell Lewis shows that a subtle use of shades and shadows can offset use of perspective in achieving a sense of depth. The relief and projection depend largely on the form and value of the shade and shadow tones. Note also the way Lewis handles the smaller detail in the shadow of the cornice.

MODELING DETAIL: LEOPOLD EIDLITZ AND WELLES BOSWORTH

Ornament and Gothic structure honestly expressed are evident in this c. 1878 pencil and wash perspective of the Assembly corridor of the New York State Capital in Albany. A dramatic perspective is achieved by the low horizon line. Leopold Eidlitz, designing only in the medieval styles, made this drawing 9½″ × 14⅝″ (24 × 37 cm).

Courtesy Avery Library, Columbia University, New York, New York.

The rough and irregular sculptural surfaces of the familiar Sphinx are rendered here by Welles Bosworth with a rare fidelity. The remarkable modeling of the subject is especially evident in the detail (reproduced at the actual size of the original) if it is viewed from a distance of several feet. Bosworth is known for the original buildings at the Massachusetts Institute of Technology, all designed in the early twentieth century from his Parisian atelier. Whether he traveled to Egypt to spend the many hours in the hot sun to complete this drawing is not known.

CHAPTER SEVEN
INTERIORS AND FURNITURE

This topic is very important to designers when you consider how many portray room interiors, furniture, and furnishings in the course of their work. Consider also how many artists draw interiors for advertisements or stories in magazines and newspapers. Architects are among the many other professionals who need to know how to delineate room interiors and their accessories.

Many of these professionals—whether they work in pencil or some other medium—use certain conventions of representation that have gradually been developed over the years. These representations must, however, be based on the natural appearance of actual interiors, so first you need to become familiar with such spaces.

INTERIORS ARE STILL-LIFES

It is obvious that an interior is simply an enlarged type of still-life. Complete interiors are much bigger than most still-life subjects, however, so they demand a greater knowledge of drawing and particularly of the principles of perspective.

PERSPECTIVE

When you draw a still-life, the entire subject falls completely within your range of vision. It is not necessary to shift the eye in order to take it in. In dealing with any major portion of a room, however, you are forced to shift your gaze as you draw and you are unable to see the entire subject distinctly at one time.

As a result unless you are so familiar with perspective principles that you can reconcile all the conflicting shapes in your drawing, you are likely to develop a sort of composite effect that may be all wrong. Therefore work into the subject gradually, selecting only a corner or some other limited area of a room as the subject of your first drawing.

In subsequent drawings gradually take in more and more until you feel qualified to handle as much as can be viewed from any one point. If problems of perspective arise, review the related material in Chapter 5.

INTERIOR LIGHTING

Indoor lighting is quite different from outdoor lighting. In the open, light normally comes from a single source—the sun—in rays that can be considered parallel. So if the artist locates that source, knowing that all light rays come from that direction and cast shadows consistently in that direction, the problem is half solved.

Indoors, however, even in those cases where actual sunlight is pouring into the room through one or more openings, a great amount of light will radiate at different angles, only to be reflected from surface to surface in a complicated fashion. This lighting will affect the value, form, and direction of shadows, some being light and some dark, with certain edges sharply defined and others indistinct. A chair leg, for example, often casts several shadows on the floor at once and a lighting fixture as many more on the wall or ceiling.

This is further complicated by numerous reflections, which will be discussed in a moment. Notwithstanding all this, the fact that such complex conditions exist frequently works to the advantage of the more experienced artist, who is able to arrange values almost as he or she chooses.

As a rule it is best not to begin by drawing every little change in tone that you see, but by simplifying the whole, working for the general effect in a broad, direct manner. When you enter a room you are not conscious of all the detail. So why draw it?

Because much interior lighting is indirect and the light rays diffused, the general effect is usually softer than in an exterior in direct light. The tones blend or merge into one another and the division between light and shade is less clearly defined.

This indefinite effect can be desirable in certain drawings, but it can be easily carried to extremes, resulting in a displeasing effect. This kind of drawing can be so gray and lacking in contrast that it is hardly suitable, where a drawing with clean edges and sharp definition of tone is preferred as a rule to a soft, vague interpretation.

If you work for a crisp result you will find that many objects found in interiors, being well polished and smooth, offer strong reflections and highlights that, if carefully used, serve as a pleasing break in the grayness of the general effect. Outdoors you seldom find such shiny surfaces, with the exception of smooth water and glass, since building materials are usually rather dull in finish.

Materials found indoors, on the other hand, often exhibit the opposite characteristics. Floors are highly polished wood or marble; the trim is frequently varnished or given some enamel finish; and glazed tiles, linoleum, or other shiny materials are often used. Especially in furniture and in such accessories as lighting fixtures and vases, you find many surfaces of high reflective value. Table tops, for example, frequently act almost like mirrors, while the glass in the framed pictures on the walls has similar characteristics. Chair arms, door knobs, clocks, dishes all add little highlights, often of extreme brillance in relation to the surroundings.

These sharply contrasting accents give life to your work, especially drawings of an architectural nature. Many otherwise "dead" drawings receive most of their character from just such accents.

LIGHTING AND COMPOSITION

Many interior drawings fall into two categories: those in which the artist stands with his or her back to the light, drawing a lighted area (such as a room corner away from a window), and those in which the artist faces the light. The second position usually results in more dramatic compositions. Not only are the window sashes and frames often thrown into sharp silhouette against the light, but objects near the window will show striking contrasts of light, shade, and shadow.

TEXTURES AND DETAILS

Aside from these basic considerations, there are many secondary problems that need your attention. Take textures, for instance. Interiors offer an amazing variety: the roughness of stonework and brickwork; the smoothness of mirrors, window glass, and other glossy surfaces; such endless woven fabrics as rugs, upholstery, wall hangings. Ultimately, you must be prepared to portray nearly every material in almost every form.

To draw draperies or upholstery materials, for example, it is necessary to carefully observe the various fabrics used for such purposes, studying each with care, looking at it up close and at a distance, in bright and subdued light, laid out smoothly and draped in folds. Search always for the material's special characteristics under all these conditions, and try to retain mental impressions of these peculiarities for future use. Then

Figure 1. Note the suggestive treatment of detail and the shadows cast on the floor; and practice in this informal manner. Be sure to work in a scale larger than shown here.

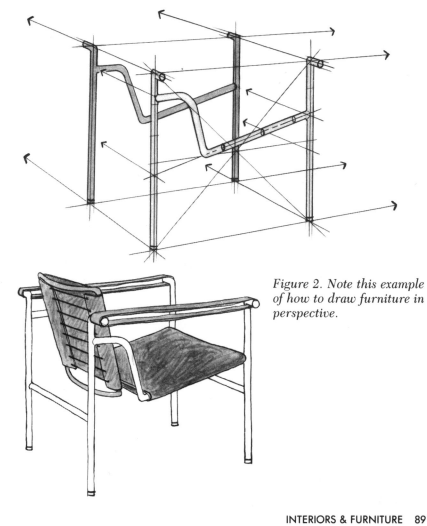

Figure 2. Note this example of how to draw furniture in perspective.

compare one fabric with another or drape several in such a way that they can be easily seen at one time.

It is surprising what differences you can discover by this sort of inspection and analysis. A piece of satin and a piece of cotton of similar color and tone will vary greatly in appearance. Even a light piece of cotton and a dark piece of the same material will show markedly dissimilar effects, in addition to contrast in color. Light-colored cloth usually shows more contrast in values than darker material of a similar kind because the dark color seems to absorb many of the lighter values of shade and shadow.

A smooth material with a sheen will not look at all like some dull fabric of similar tone since it will have many highlights and reflections. Certain fabrics, such as velours, will sometimes appear dark where you expect them to be light and light where other materials would be dark. By rubbing the nap, you can change the effect from light to dark or dark to light instantly.

Many materials of a shiny nature grow dull and soft with age, but there are exceptions. Others—leather, for example—often become smooth and glossy with wear. The smoother the material, the more complicated and changeable its values are as a rule and the stronger its highlights.

Among draping fabrics that is great variety in the way they hang; some are stiff and inflexible and others soft and yielding. Heavy materials usually hang quite straight and show fewer small folds and creases than the ones that are light in weight. Heavy materials are also generally opaque. For this reason they are sometimes less difficult to represent than thin nets, scrims, and similar fabrics that are so translucent or even transparent that they show light or sometimes objects through them.

INDIVIDUAL PIECES OF FURNITURE

Ordinarily the greatest difficulty in getting the perspective of interiors correct comes not in handling the architectural background, which is usually quite simple, but in placing and representing the furniture. To

Figure 3. Notice the treatment of the various textures found indoors: brickwork, plaster, beams, and polished floor in particular. When drawing a surface such as a shiny floor or table top, show some lines representing the reflections of objects and other lines, often in the opposite direction, indicating the surfaces of the boards themselves.

draw furniture well—correct in itself and at the same time right in relation to the rest of the room—is far from easy. In many drawings the individual pieces look too large or small or seem tipped, wrongly foreshortened, or otherwise incorrect in some way.

For this reason it is often best to start practicing with single pieces of furniture. Fortunately models are always available wherever you choose to begin. In fact chairs are extremely good for first practice. As a rule they look best if shown some distance away, so place each across the room before sketching.

The various pieces of furniture shown in Figures 1 and 2 were handled crisply and directly and offer many helpful hints. Note the sug-

gestive treatment of the detail: You don't need to add much to establish the idea. Also note the shadows cast on the floor by most of the pieces in Figure 1. Such shadows serve to "hold down" furniture, preventing any effect of floating in space.

Study these drawings individually. You will discover that there are differences in the treatment used. While all these sketches show a dark object against a light background, you might consider when it would be effective to use a light-against-dark value arrangement.

DRAWING FOR PRACTICE

As soon as you have carefully studied the appearance of the many textures found in interiors and practiced draw-

ing different pieces of furniture, you will be ready to attempt some drawings, giving special attention to surfaces and textures.

Arrange compositions of several objects that are commonly associated by use and that also offer a variety of surfaces. Old objects are especially good for this sort of practice, since the textures of antiques are more varied and interesting than those of many modern pieces.

Arrange an easy chair, a table, and a reading lamp, for instance, to form a pleasing group, adding perhaps a book, magazine, or other accessories that might complete the composition. Have the light coming from one direction, if this is practical, to avoid complicated shadows.

Figure 4. Many of the lines drawn first with instruments were allowed to remain in this meticulous rendering by J. Pauli.

When drawing, use great care in suggesting such things as the shine of the table top and the floor, the numerous touches of highlight, and the texture of the rug and the lampshade. Try to emphasize the center of interest. Also pay special attention to the edges, separating the light from the shade and making them clean-cut when they appear so and indefinite where such an effect seems called for. If you find this practice too difficult, work from photographs, selecting those clearly showing detail. (See Chapter 9, "Drawing from Photographs," for further discussion.)

SEVERAL EXAMPLES

A few examples of how interiors can be rendered are included in this section. Study the various techniques used to give different moods to each space.

Figure 3 shows how to treat such textures as brickwork, rough plaster, hewn beams, and polished floor. When drawing a surface such as a shiny floor or table top, show some lines representing the reflections of objects and other lines, often in the opposite direction, indicating the surfaces of the boards themselves. A study of the floor shown here reveals both these sets of lines.

The drawing by J. Pauli in Figure 4 shows an entirely different handling: The drawing was carefully blocked out with instruments and finished freehand in pencil with infinite care. Some of the mechanical lines were allowed to show. Such drawings are often used in catalogs where furniture, lighting fixtures, office equipment, or the like are advertised.

Note how A. Thornton Bishop has paid careful attention to natural values in Figure 5. Here a complete range of tone has been used, with a considerable amount of black. As noted elsewhere, you get far greater richness of tone—a suggestion of actual color—when black is used than when you depend solely on gray and white. Gray drawings are almost always inclined to be a bit dull and heavy.

The drawing in Figure 5 also has a fine sense of depth and distance, accomplished largely by the converging perspective lines. Much depth is gained too by the way in which the contrasts have been arranged. The

Figure 5. Consistency between technique and subject is one characteristic of this pleasing drawing by A. Thornton Bishop. The contrasting "spotting" of the lights and the darks produces life and sparkle.

Figure 6. Note the strong center of interest, the variety of line, and the clever indication of material in this drawing of a plaster chimney in Somerset, England, by Sydney R. Jones.

Figure 7. It's important to try your hand at rendering elevations until you can match the work of Richard M. Powers shown here.

Figure 8. Outline, gray wash, and areas of black are effectively combined in this stylized handling by Verna Salomonsky. Compare this with the plan of this room in Figure 10.

table top and the two chairs at the left have been kept comparatively light against a darker background, bringing them forward, while the backs of the two opposite chairs have been forced a bit to make them dark against the light pedestal of the pilaster beyond and light against the shadow of the dropleaf table. Only by working for contrasts of this sort can you bring objects forward or carry them back at will.

Now note the carefully treated study by Sydney R. Jones in Figure 6. This rendering, like the last one, makes use of black, though here it is largely confined to a single area within the fireplace opening. This one dark accent, seen in relief against the white around it, makes the fireplace a strong center of interest for the entire sketch. The converging

perspective lines of the ceiling beams and flagstones also help carry the eye to this center.

Not only has this drawing an easily understood composition, but technically it has much to teach. Observe the great variety of strokes. There are the long and unbroken lines of the ceiling, for instance, which were of course much longer in the original than as reproduced here.

Then just below them minute dots are visible along the cornice. Note too the numerous dots by which the moldings surrounding the coat of arms of the overmantel are formed, some of them so tiny in this reproduction that they are almost lost. Notice likewise the speckling of the fireback behind the andirons.

Between these small dots and the long lines of the ceiling you can find

great variety in both length and character of stroke. Crosshatching has been used sparingly in some of the shadow tones. Outline has scarcely been used by itself, but it has been added to reinforce many of the edges. Note the vertical boundaries of the chimney breast, for instance.

DRAWING ELEVATIONS AND PLANS

The architect or interior designer should now be acquainted with several methods of representing various types of interiors drawn in perspective, as the above examples have shown. He or she should also acquire skill in delineating elevations and plans.

Figure 7 is an elevation of a simple interior by Richard M. Powers. In

Figure 9. Here Verna Salomonsky expresses a room's essential features adequately and pleasingly by simple means.

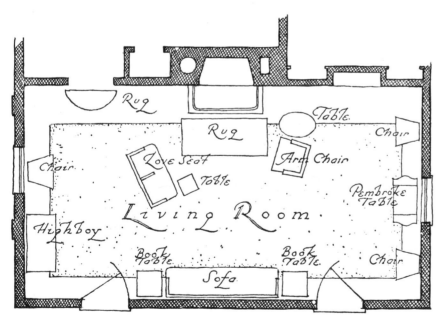

Figure 10. This treatment of the plan for Figure 8, also by Verna Salomonsky, is simple, adequate, and pleasing.

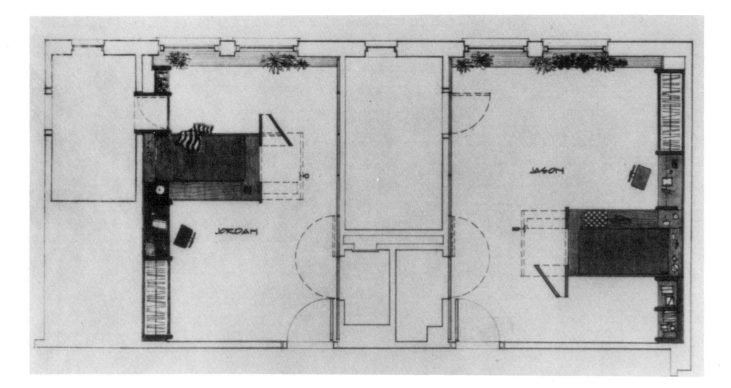

Figure 11. Norman Diekman's plan (above) and perspective (below) for a bedroom are used interdependently for presentation and discussion with a client. (Designed by William Machado and Norman Diekman.)

drawing elevations the most difficult thing is expressing depth; without traditional perspective aiding the viewer, it is sometimes difficult to interpret. This fact must therefore always be foremost in the artist's or designer's mind.

A plan, on the other hand, is more diagrammatic as a rule and may be treated in a more conventional way. The room by Verna Salomonsky in Figure 8 is interesting in this respect. An actual plan for this room is shown in Figure 10.

Plans are also a useful way to lay out alternatives for discussion with clients. This may involve alternate plan schemes, minor variations in plan that need to be resolved, or various furniture arrangements possible within a particular space. Norman Diekman shows in Figure 11 plans for two children's rooms, with the elements, sizes, shapes, and locations of the special built-in units planned. Because the intended upper and lower bunk beds and elevated playhouse are quite unusual, the perspective below makes these arrangements absolutely clear.

The pair of plans shown in Figure 12 may appear identical at first glance, but they include small differences. The plan on right shows a floor pattern with staggered joint lines, with the informal seating group arranged in a free, nearly circular pattern. Drapery is indicated as the means of controlling the sun, light, and view that the huge window area implies. In the plan on the left the floor pattern has become a grid of squares and the seating group is more formal, the plant is relocated, and the drapery has vanished. The only other changes are a few minor exchanges of small tables. By showing these changes in plan clients can quickly and easily consider the impact of changes in the actual space.

PEN AND WASH

Sometimes when a pen drawing is not wholly successful in and of itself a wash of some gray watercolor or diluted ink may be applied to it or parts of it with exciting results. Or you may deliberately combine ink and wash, treating the entire drawing in a somewhat sketchy way.

A conventional combination of the two media is shown in the drawings by Verna Salomonsky (Figures 8 through 10). In most drawings of this type areas of solid black give the necessary accent. The possible combinations are almost limitless. Be careful, however, where you place the blacks. They must be arranged with the greatest care or they will destroy the balance of the composition or attract too much attention to nonessentials.

All these examples have solved this problem and should be studied with care. As a rule objects are first outlined in ink; then the blacks are added, the ink applied with either pen or brush; and finally the gray washes are laid in with a few simple values. Often these washes are flat or graded in the simplest possible way.

In this chapter some of the most common kinds of interior drawings have been discussed in a general way, though you should seek many examples to supplement what is offered here. A gallery of examples follows with a wide range of treatments and subjects.

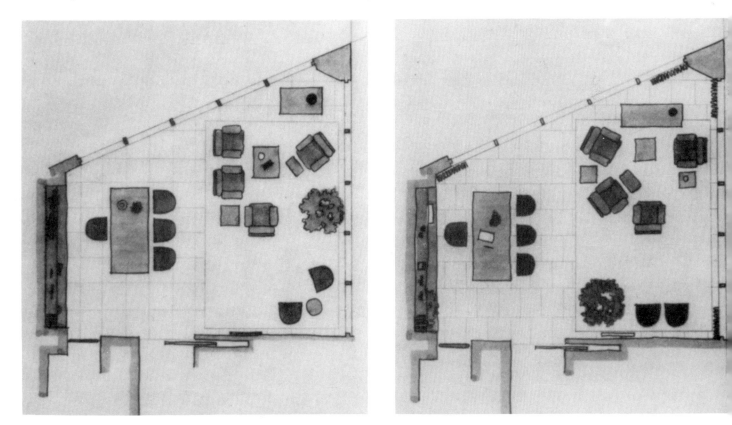

Figure 12. Various furniture layouts can be explored quickly by drawing on overlays of tracing paper, using an architectural plan below.

EXAMPLES

The architectural interior can be simple and powerful or finely detailed, ornamented, and delicate; conceived as a neutral backdrop or as a strong dramatic statement; well lit or subdued; cluttered with furniture and bric-a-brac, or streamlined, with all but seating and tables tucked out of sight. Study the examples on the following pages for the wide range of effects seasoned designers and artists have been able to achieve using subtleties of line, tone, and texture to evoke the personality of each space.

The great sense of strength of Santa Maria Maggiore in Rome is captured here by P. M. Letarouilly, who combined an intense buildup of ink linework with a powerful one-point perspective that draws your eye to the arch of triumph, high altar, and baldachino. Also by rendering the floor and columns only lightly, but applying heavy tone to the upper level walls and the coffered ceiling, the artist portrays the great height of this fifth-century basilica. People and floor pattern abet the sense of great scale of the interior. The drawing first appeared in *Edifices de Rome Moderne*, published in 1868.

(Page 100) The dense texture of lines pulls the eye upward to the great fan vault of the ante-chapel at King's College in Cambridge. The same technique was used by Letarouilly at Santa Maria Maggiore (page 98). This drawing by F. MacKenzie of the Perpendicular style chapel (completed in 1515) is from J. Britton's *Architectural Antiquities of Great Britain.*, published between 1807 and 1826.

(Page 101) A sharp pencil, a dramatic viewing point, and appropriate use of scale elements helped Helmut Jacoby express the soaring height of this Philip Johnson proposal for a Washington Place arcade in New York City, an exciting interior space that reminds one of John Paxton's iron and glass Crystal Palace of 1851. Planters, people, tables, and the dividers in the vertical support trusses all serve to point up the great height of the space.

THE POWER OF ONE-POINT PERSPECTIVE:
P. M. LETAROUILLY

CREATING SCALE THROUGH TEXTURE: F. MACKENZIE

EVOKING TALL SPACES:
HELMUT JACOBY FOR PHILIP JOHNSON

EXERCISES IN IMAGINATION: WALTER GROPIUS

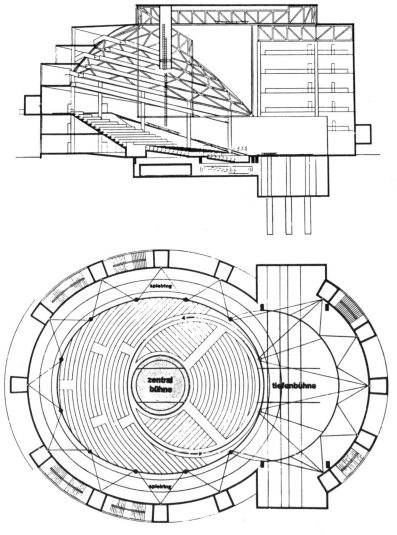

Walter Gropius, a founder of the modern movement in architecture, felt compelled to reexamine and redesign every building type in the light of modern materials and building techniques, as well as social and cultural needs. He often failed to have such schemes built, but that never discouraged him. One such example is the "total theater" he designed for Berlin in 1927. The theater did away with the proscenium arch, and half the seats could be rotated to create a central stage. The section and floor plan, as well as the rough ink sketch by Gropius, show the stage in the center position.

Jammed with shoppers everyday, Moscow's "GUM" Department Store (or State Universal Store, known locally as just "Goom") seems to be the ultimate in department stores. A vast Victorian complex reminiscent of an oriental bazaar, its unique features are the iron stairways, balconies, and bridges joining three huge floors. This drawing by Paul Hogarth done in 1969 with a Faber 702 sketching pencil is but one of fifty in a 15″ × 20″ (38 × 51 cm) sketchbook of Glastonbury Antique drawing paper.
   From *A Russian Journey: From Suzdal to Samarkand*, 1969. Courtesy Cassell and Company, London; and Hill & Wang, Inc., New York.

INTERPRETING A FEELING: PAUL HOGARTH

Moscow: GUM
Department Store

EFFECTS WITH NATURAL LIGHT: PAUL RUDOLPH

EXPLORING A CHANGE OF DIRECTION: JAMES COOTE

CAPTURING MOVEMENT WITH LINE: LE CORBUSIER

A highly intricate network of foot and automobile traffic marked this grand but unbuilt 1931 scheme by Le Corbusier for the Palace of the Soviets in Moscow. Using a deceptively simple technique of line, texture, and dramatic two-point perspective, the architect hints at great spaces and sweeping movement in this entrance lobby and assembly space for a hall to seat 6,500 delegates. Even though no ceiling is shown, a sense of height is created by the pattern of levels and ramps.

(Page 104) This 1968 project for a chapel at Tuskegee Institute in Tuskegee, Alabama, shows the dramatic effect natural light can have on a majestic interior. Paul Rudolph drew the perspective to show the owner what he hoped to achieve in the final building. Although the project was never built, the drawing nonetheless strongly attests to Rudolph's conception of interior spaces. Drawn after the view was first worked out in a preparatory outline, the work, approximately 30" × 20" (76 × 51 cm), was done in ink on white Strathmore paper.

(Page 105) This 1981 study sketch for the Kilgore House in Austin, Texas, combines a reflected ceiling plan at the top with a perspective. The 14" × 17" (36 × 43 cm) pencil drawing on white tracing paper was done very quickly by architect James Coote, who wanted to explore a 45° change of direction and a level change in the plan. Coote was also using the drawing to study the Robert Adam-derived ceiling and the relative scale of the bookcase at the left and the fireplace at the right. Preferring white tracing paper to yellow, which he finds distracting, Coote likes the suggestiveness, softness, and responsiveness of graphite.

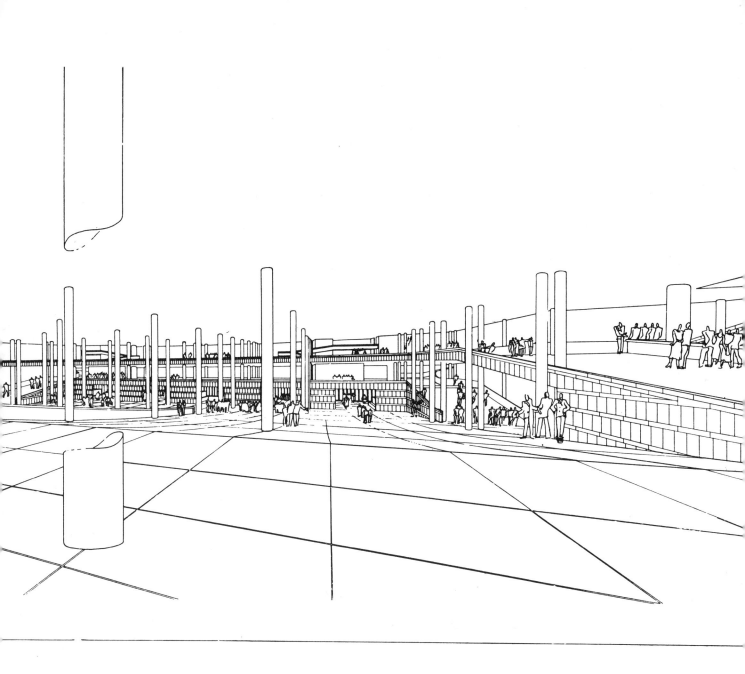

WHEN PLAN AND SECTION ARE NOT ENOUGH: BARTHOLOMEW VOORSANGER AND EDWARD MILLS

Because they had to submit drawings of what the San-paolo Bank's New York office would actually look like to the bank's headquarters in Turin, Italy, Voorsanger and Mills developed these drawings for the final schematic phase of the project in May 1980. Mere plans and sections would not have conveyed this complex design, as planes and spaces unfold and reconnect in a continuous sequence. Sketches were first drawn on yellow tracing paper and then traced over in ink on Mylar with a 00 and 000 Kohl-I-Noor Rapidograph. Each sketch is about 6″ × 6″ (15 × 15 cm), with four drawings fitting on a 16″ × 16″ (41 × 41 cm) sheet of paper.

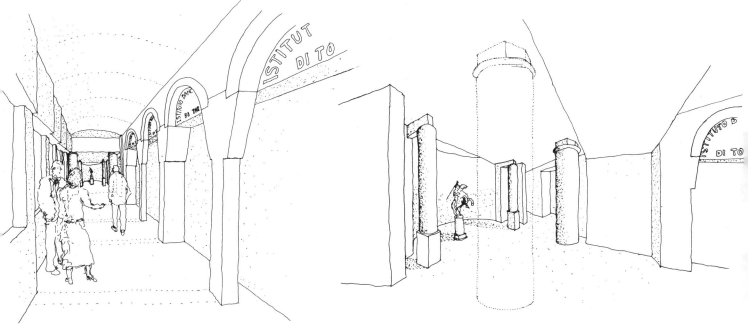

SWIFT STROKES TO CAPTURE SPACE AND SCALE: ALVAR AALTO

Pen on tracing paper evokes the character of this interior (right) and longitudinal section (below) of Alvar Aalto's Church of Vouksenniska in Imatra, Finland. The section, which is about 10″ × 5½″ (25 × 13 cm), including base and guidelines, served to study the ceiling form of this church, including a skylight. Short, rapid strokes of the pen and limited use of tone helped the architect define at a small scale the essential space features of the design. The 1958 drawing was first included in a student publication at North Carolina State University at Raleigh and published by the University of North Carolina Press.

THE THUMBNAIL SKETCH: NORMAN DIEKMAN

Norman Diekman used pen and ink on a white paper placemat to explore an arrangement of table and chairs near a dining room window. He sought to evoke a mood of long leisurely meals at a large window that looks out over the ocean, with ships of all sizes passing by—a place to talk or dream. The upper sketch was done fast, to loosen the hand; the lower sketch is a refinement, with added tone and linework. Each sketch is about 5″ × 4″ (13 × 10 cm).

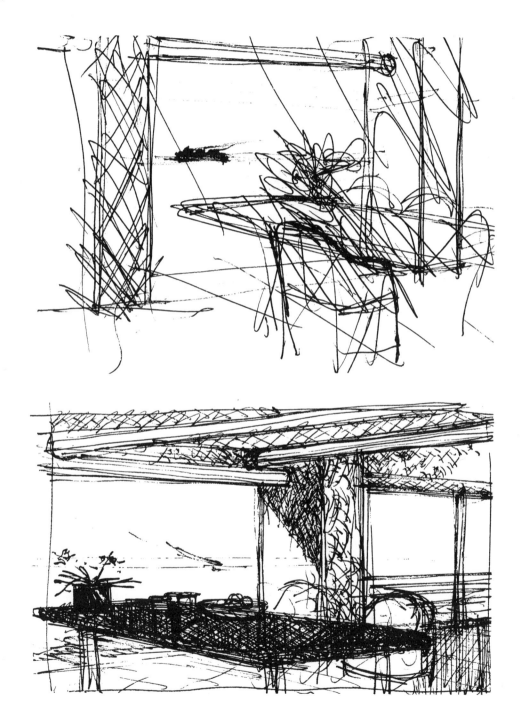

LINKING SPACE, ART, AND FURNITURE: FLORENCE KNOLL BASSETT

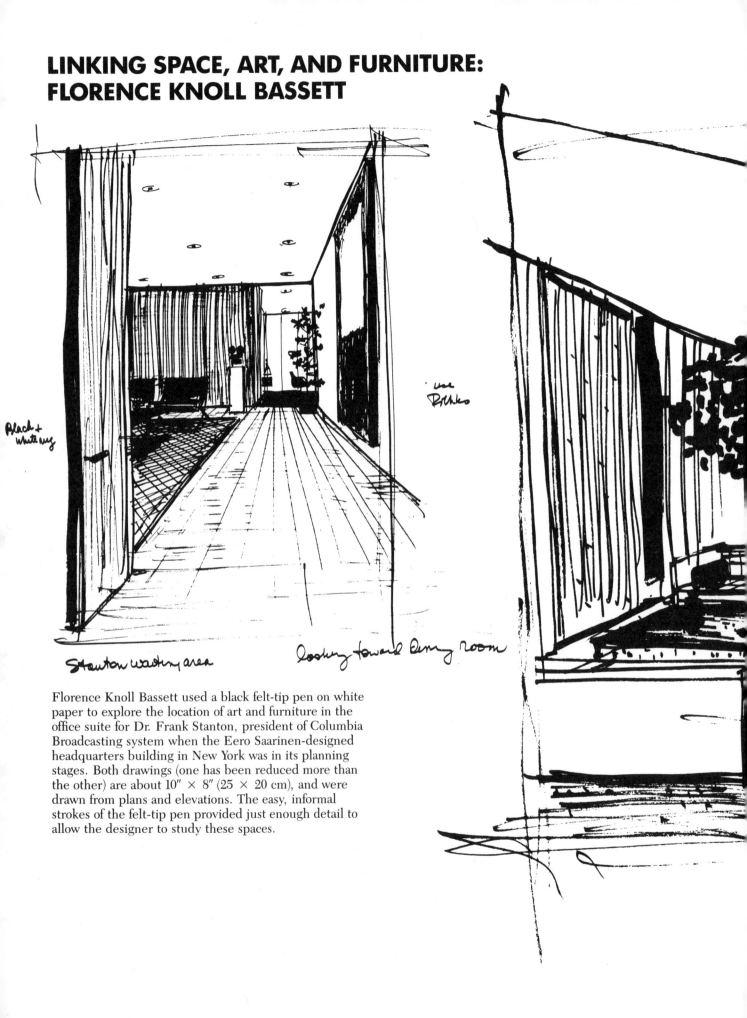

Black + white rug

use Rothko

Stanton waiting area

looking toward dining room

Florence Knoll Bassett used a black felt-tip pen on white paper to explore the location of art and furniture in the office suite for Dr. Frank Stanton, president of Columbia Broadcasting system when the Eero Saarinen-designed headquarters building in New York was in its planning stages. Both drawings (one has been reduced more than the other) are about 10″ × 8″ (25 × 20 cm), and were drawn from plans and elevations. The easy, informal strokes of the felt-tip pen provided just enough detail to allow the designer to study these spaces.

CHAPTER EIGHT
LANDSCAPE AND CITYSCAPE

The setting for the building you draw, whether it's in the country or part of a city street, is a crucial element in your drawing—and in many ways the hardest to do well. The best approach is to break down the surroundings into the various elements, study them, learn how to express them in their various seasons, states, and moods, and then bring them together methodically in your final drawing.

This chapter will show you how to draw trees, various kinds and conditions of water (both liquid and frozen), skies, clouds, and fog, along with hints on how to relate all these to the buildings themselves.

DRAWING TREES

If you draw buildings in their original landscapes, sooner or later you are going to draw trees. In this chapter certain aspects of the tree that are needed to make convincing-looking drawings will be discussed.

All trees are basically made up of the trunk, branches, and crown. When you first draw the tree, look at the simplified silhouette, the relationship of the trunk to the branches, the area between the trunk and the crown, the sky holes (open areas) to the larger masses of the crown, and so on.

While a portrait painter will measure the distance between the eyes, nose, mouth, and so on, the landscape artist must measure the proportion between the height to the width, how far up the trunk the branches begin, the thickness of the trunk to the main branches, and the main branches to the ends of the branch. This may seem obvious to you, but trees are poorly drawn for two rea-

sons: the silhouette is not interesting (it looks like a lollipop), and the trunk is either too large or too small for the crown.

It is important, however, not to make up a tree or use a stereotype tree, but go out and actually draw a tree that you can identify. In this chapter the different types of trees and the principal steps in drawing them will be discussed.

Types of Trees. While it isn't necessary to know every type of tree, there are three basic groups that it's helpful to be able to identify: (1) broadleafs, which include the elm, maple, oak, sycamore, willow, among many others; (2) conifers, which include the fir, pine, and spruce; and (3) palms, which include the coconut, jade, and palmetto.

There are many more examples of trees in each of the tree groups. However, if you understand the basic approach and characteristics of each group, you should be able to draw all types of trees.

Principal Steps in Drawing Trees. Since each tree is unique, look for the character of the tree you are about to draw. There are four basic things to note before you begin drawing.

The General Shape. Look at the overall shape of the tree. One way to do this is by taking an imaginary piece of plastic wrap and completely enclosing the tree. When you look at a tree in this way, all the intricate outlines are reduced to a simple, flat pattern. Into this flat pattern the smaller, individual branches can be fitted. This is true whether you are

drawing a tree in the summer with all its leaves or in the winter when just the skelton is visible.

The Silhouette. The next step is to determine the silhouette. A careful study of the silhouette is important because it gives you the individual character of the tree. Each tree looks different because the silhouette of each tree is different. In the silhouette you can see the number as well as the size of the sky holes, the branches that extend farther than others, and the bare branches where there are no leaves.

The Width and Height Proportion. The proportion of the width to the height is very important. Check the height with the width by simply squaring off the tree, using your pencil to measure. With your arm fully extended and your pencil in a horizontal position, line up the top of the pencil with one side of the tree and move your fingers up the pencil until they mark the other side of the tree. This length on the pencil corresponds to the width of the tree.

Without shifting your fingers, turn the pencil to an upright position, keeping your arm fully extended. You can then see the relationship of the width to the height. Always start with the shortest dimension first, so you can compare that with the longest.

Pattern of Lights and Darks. Before you begin rendering the tones in the tree, it is important to identify a simplified pattern of lights and darks. Make sure there is a definite area of light and dark. Try to keep these areas separate so that there are no lights in the dark area and darks in the light area.

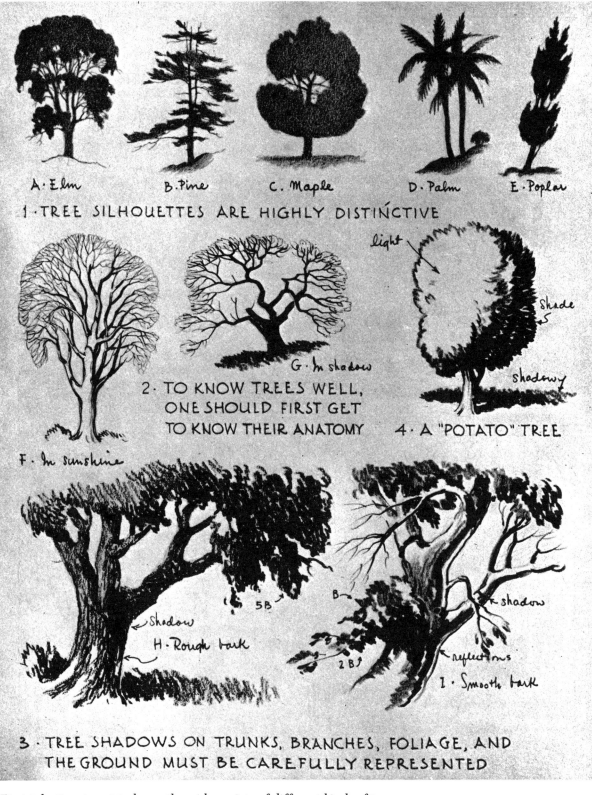

A. Elm   B. Pine   C. Maple   D. Palm   E. Poplar

1 · TREE SILHOUETTES ARE HIGHLY DISTINCTIVE

G · In shadow

2 · TO KNOW TREES WELL, ONE SHOULD FIRST GET TO KNOW THEIR ANATOMY

light

shade

shadowy

4 · A "POTATO" TREE

F · In sunshine

Shadow
5B
H · Rough bark

B

shadow

reflections

2B

I · Smooth bark

3 · TREE SHADOWS ON TRUNKS, BRANCHES, FOLIAGE, AND THE GROUND MUST BE CAREFULLY REPRESENTED

First take time to get to know the wide variety of different kinds of trees. Careful study will show you that their basic form can often be depicted by silhouette alone.

Broadleaf trees

The general shape

The silhouette

The width and height proportion

Pattern of lights or darks

Conifer trees

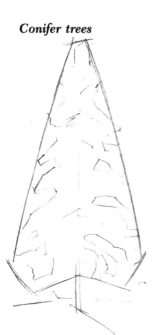

The general shape

The silhouette

The width and height proportion

Pattern of lights and darks

Palm trees

The general shape

The silhouette

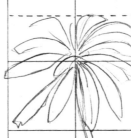

The width and height proportion

Pattern of lights and darks

Trunks

This rendering shows two types of tree trunks. As you draw trunks, keep in mind their shape. All trunks are basically cylinders, so create that form first with a 2H pencil. On this base draw various textures that are characteristic of the particular type of tree. Use HB and 2B pencils with short strokes to indicate the bark, with smooth and rough areas, but always keep in mind the round form underneath.

EXERCISE 1. BROADLEAFS

Make the initial sketch with a 4H pencil. The proportion between trees and houses is very important because it will give you the relative size of each. There are two points that you should establish immediately: (1) the fullness of the crown of the tree, that is, the width to the height; and (2) an indication of the shadow side and the light side. In addition to the outline of the crown, also draw some of the main branches leading out to the ends of the tree. This will indicate where some of the branches will go when you lay in the tones.

First start with the values of the tree. Use two pencils: a 4H for the light side and an HB for the dark value. Draw the *complete* tree with the 4H pencil, rendering the silhouette; be sure to note where the sky holes will be and what the edge will look like. After this, take the HB pencil and lay in the shadow side of the tree. Because the light tone is already under the dark side, leave some of the light tone showing, which will give a nice breakup of the dark area.

Now that the tree is drawn, you can start on the surrounding area. Establish most of the darks with the HB pencil. Be aware of the vignette so that you don't leave any straight, cut-out edges. With a 4H pencil, lay in the background trees and begin the foreground. Leave the light side of the house white, until you know how much detail you want to put in this area.

Indicate the reflections in the water with horizontal strokes to give the water a flat look and also to establish contrast with the vertical strokes of the grass and bushes. When the foreground, background, and tree are finished, put a tone in the light side of the house. Then draw in the roof with a 6H pencil and the shadows and detail with a 4H pencil. Because the tree is standing by itself, it remains the center of interest, even with so many dark and light values in the rest of the drawing.

Details of the Broadleaf
It is impossible and unnecessary to indicate every leaf on a tree. With short strokes going in different directions, you can, however, get the feeling of leaves without a lot of detail. Do this on both the light and the dark sides of the crown.

EXERCISE 2. CONIFERS

After you note the characteristics of the tree, sketch in the trunk first with a 4H pencil. This gives you the direction and angle of the tree, and it acts like the backbone in figure drawing. Then draw the basic shapes of the branches and indicate where the light and shadow areas occur.

With short strokes lay in all the shadow areas with an HB pencil. Try to simplify these dark patterns. In observing a tree, notice how the branches grow: Some reach skyward or down, toward or away from you. There are areas where the branches have broken off and other areas where branches never grew. With close observation and careful study you will achieve great interest in your drawing.

When the pattern of darks is established, put in the light side with a 2H pencil. The difference between the light and the dark sides should not be more than two values. On the light side the strokes should be short and fan out as the branches become smaller. Then put in all the small, broken, bare branches, connect some of the longer branches to the trunk, and add the foreground and background.

Details of the Conifer

The trunk and the bare branches are not outlines. The strokes and tones hold the shape and edges. Notice the short strokes used to indicate the needles. Be sure to make the strokes fan out on each side of the branch.

EXERCISE 3: PALMS

Sketch in the basic proportions and characteristics with a 4H pencil. Your main concern should be the length of the branches from the center, rather than the outside shape. In drawing palm trees, there is no definite shape to the crown as with broadleafs. Using an HB pencil, start the darkest tones in the center of the tree where all the branches come together. The dark side of the tree is rendered with strokes that start at the spine of the leaves. Leave some of the main branches white in the dark area.

With a 2H pencil draw in the light side of the tree, indicating the leaves in the same way as for the dark side. Where some of the branches overlap, it looks like crosshatching, which is characteristic of this type of tree.

After the leaves are completed, render the tone in the trunk with a 2H pencil, using short vertical strokes. To show roundness of the trunk, apply more pressure to the strokes on the right side. This gives you a slightly darker tone. Indicate a cast shadow near the center with an HB pencil, and also put in some horizontal lines for the bark. With a 6H pencil put in the background using one tone and very little detail. Finish the drawing with nondescript foliage in the foreground with a 2B pencil.

Details of the Palm

A. Before you start to draw a palm tree, make sure you understand how the branches extend from the main trunk. This area is relatively small, as compared with other types of trees. Notice how some branches go to the right, the left, back, and foreward.

B. There is generally a dark side and a light side to the fan shape of the leaf. By following the spine of the leaf, you can establish this characteristic of the palm.

C. Start at the spine, and draw the strokes fanning out and coming to a point at the end.

D. Indicate the basic roundness of the tree trunk before adding any texture.

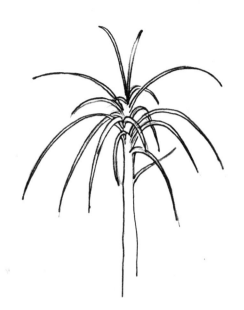

B

A

C

D

The Elm
The elm tree is a classic example of a large umbrella-shaped crown that creates
a beautiful and graceful silhouette. Once you lay in the overall shape of the
tree with accurate proportions between the crown and the trunk, draw the
entire silhouette of the crown with a 2H pencil, with the lightest tone on the
crown. On top of this draw the shadow area with an HB pencil. It isn't
necessary to completely cover the shadow side because a few missed places let
a little of the lighter tone show through.

Spidery Fingers

Probably the best time to study trees is in the winter when there are no leaves. It is interesting to see how the main trunk splits and the branches keep getting smaller and smaller as they reach the ends. Be extremely careful that all the branches do not come out from the sides of the trunk. As you draw a leafless tree, have some of the branches come toward you and some go away from you.

After laying the drawing in with a 4H pencil, start on the main trunk first and then draw the smaller branches. Using a 2H pencil, draw the trunk with strokes going in different directions. Make sure, however, to retain the basic cylinder shape. Draw the small building and fences with 2H and HB pencils, and render all accents with a 2B pencil.

Palms
Draw the large overall shape first and indicate the action of the trunk (palm trees often bend and lean due to the narrow trunk). Draw the large palm leaves from the center out to the edges with a 2H pencil, and put in all dark areas with an HB pencil. Render the trunk with many short strokes using a 4H pencil. A common characteristic of palms are horizontal lines, which you can draw in with an HB pencil.

DRAWING WATER

The characteristics of water present some of the same complications as those of glass. In fact water not only has the two important characteristics of transparency and the power to reflect images, but adds another peculiarity: its surface is constantly changing from smooth one moment, to rippled the next, to possibly choppy later if disturbed by large waves.

Smooth water often gives as perfect a reflection as a mirror, yet under slightly altered conditions the images are distorted or destroyed. Or the surface can become like a transparent pane of glass, with the bottom plainly visible. Water can also appear opaque and lifeless when only the surface is visible.

Water's appearance and changes are due in part to three conditions: (1) the depth, color, and purity of the water; (2) the point from which it is viewed; (3) the angle at which rays of light reach its surface. Deep, pure water, for instance, is usually an almost perfect mirror if it is still, especially if you look *along* it rather than down on it from above. But in a shallow or muddy pool the reflected images are often merged or blended with the tone of the water itself or distorted by refraction, with the tone of the bottom showing through.

If you look directly down on water it seems far more

Figure 1. The water in this photograph is absolutely motionless.

Figure 2. The slight motion of the water disrupts the reflections.

transparent than when viewed in a more nearly horizontal direction. This is true whether it is smooth or rather rough. When light rays reach the surface at some angles, reflections that otherwise exist may disappear, and the effect of transparency is lost also, with the surface appearing opaque.

This goes for calm water. Let the slightest breeze ruffle the surface and the complications are still greater. And each change in the force or direction of the wind causes a still different effect. These things all show how impossible it is to give definite rules on rendering water. Only personal observation and practice will bring you any real proficiency in its treatment.

There are, however, a few suggestions that may help you. First be sure to correctly draw the lines bounding any body of water. Unless you do this, distortion may occur, with the water seeming to slope or bend in an unnatural manner. In a large lake or sea, where the farther shore is invisible because it is so far away, the horizon line of the water coincides with the eye level of any visible buildings. Occasionally, however, you can move this line up or down a bit, if it helps you obtain a better composition. In smaller bodies, the distant shore lines also appear practically horizontal. Once the outline is correct, block in whatever definite reflections there may be, drawing them with great care.

Calm Water. You might expect that calm water would be easy to represent, but this is not necessarily the case. In fact calm water can be very difficult, for it often acts like a mirror reflecting the sky, nearby trees, buildings, boats, people—demanding that each of these things be drawn in duplicate.

If the water is perfectly calm and clear, these reflections may be so distinct that they can prove as hard to do as the objects themselves—possibly harder, because perplexing perspective problems are often involved. Reflections seldom seem to be *exact* facsimiles of the objects reflected (note Figure 1). Such inverted images must be represented with a certain dash too, in order to indicate the flatness, smoothness, and liquidity of the water.

Sometimes horizontal strokes seem called for, as a means of indicating the flatness of the surface (see Figure 3). Again, vertical lines can be successful (see Figure 4). In the latter case a few horizontal pencil lines or erased streaks (to interrupt the reflections slightly) can suggest both the flatness and the mobility of the water.

As to values, reflections sometimes match almost exactly the tone of the objects reflected (Figure 2), though more often they are slightly darker (Figure 1). Occasionally they may be lighter.

Although the usual way to master reflections on calm water is by sketching them outdoors, you can learn a few basics indoor by laying a mirror horizontally, then placing small objects upon it, and studying the shape and values of each object and its reflection. You can even make a realistic model, using sand, wax, or whatever's handy.

The little sketch at (1) in Figure 5 is typical of smooth water reflection. Here it was drawn mainly with slanting strokes, while the water as a whole was dashed in with horizontal strokes or bands (done with both pencil and eraser).

Ruffled Water. The minute the least bit of movement is set up in water, reflections become distorted, much as they would in a series of slightly curved mirrors. Yet these reflections are constantly in a state of flux. Often they appear elongated and curved, but they never assume the identical form twice in a row. You must learn these complex conditions first hand by observing moving water.

At (2) in Figure 5 is a drawing of how the reflection is affected by water that is slightly disturbed. The challenge here is how to suggest the mobility of the water with a minimum of modulation in the surface flatness. Note that the total vertical length of the reflection has become longer than before.

If tiny waves start to form—waves not large enough to destroy the reflected images entirely—some of them may be tipped in a way that catches momentary reflections of the sky or distant objects. These new reflections, merging with the old, can easily result in a sort of jigsaw puzzle of constantly altering patterns.

Waves. As water breaks into waves, any definite mirrored images of nearby objects tend to fly to bits. Each wave comes into being only to vanish again, its form, as emphasized by light and shade, constantly varying throughout the wave's brief existence. Not that the water ever entirely loses its reflective quality during this process, for its general values (and color) are still affected by such influences as the sky.

Although there are exceptions—depending on the angle of illumination—waves are quite certain (despite their light and shade) to appear generally dark when heavy clouds hang low, light when light clouds float high, and brilliant like sunlight itself when they mirror direct sunlight.

But any definite reflections of nearby objects, such as those that exist when water is calm or slightly ruffled, are transformed as soon as waves form. The reflections become indefinite, broken, even kaleidoscopic, alternately merging with and separating from the ever-changing tones of the waves' light and shade. [At (3) in Figure 5 is one representation of wave formations.]

Does all this seem complex? Well, it *is* complex. But it's not over yet. Water, whether rough or smooth, also has its own intrinsic tone—its local value. And when water is shallow, things beneath may show through to modify it. Only practice will help you capture the constantly changing qualities of water.

In the whole field of representational drawing there is perhaps nothing more difficult than water. It is not enough to portray its surface as it may appear at some given moment; you must strive to suggest the mighty power of the shifting mass beneath, as well as its weight, depth, fluidity, and rhythmic motion.

Running Water. In drawing running water you must observe rapids, waterfalls, and so on. Usually, swift water can be interpreted with quickly drawn strokes, dashed in to suggest the rapid motion. At (1) in Figure 6 is a simple representation.

In rendering this drawing, incidentally, a little technical trick was used that has many applications. For the water to appear sharp against the background, a sheet of

Figure 3. Horizontal strokes indicate the flatness of the water's surface.

Figure 4. Vertical strokes can also be used to represent reflections on the water's surface.

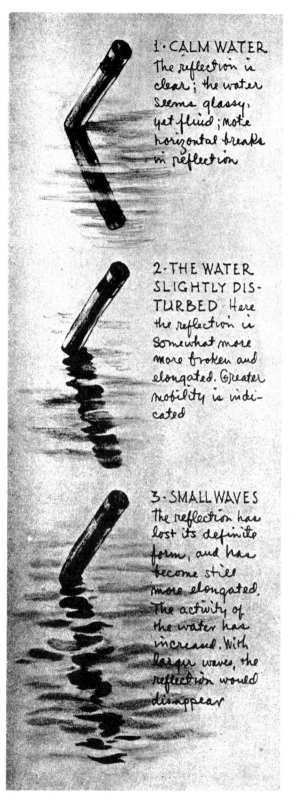

1. CALM WATER The reflection is clear; the water seems glassy, yet fluid; note horizontal breaks in reflection

2. THE WATER SLIGHTLY DISTURBED. Here the reflection is somewhat more broken and elongated. Greater mobility is indicated

3. SMALL WAVES The reflection has lost its definite form, and has become still more elongated. The activity of the water has increased. With larger waves, the reflection would disappear

Figure 5. Making comparative studies of reflections on different kinds of water can help you draw them accurately.

heavy tracing paper was cut with a curved edge to fit curve *a* exactly. The tracing paper was then laid over the water area as a shield.

The pencil lines used to build up the background tone *b* were drawn off over the edge of this shield, which was protecting the water area underneath. A similar shield was next fitted to curve *c*, and tone *d* was drawn. By these simple means the water was made to stand out sharply against its background.

Wet Surfaces. The artist is concerned not only with mobile bodies of water like lakes, seas, or streams, but with all sorts of wet surfaces. A wet sidewalk, roof, or awning takes on much the character of a mirror [see (2) in Figure 6]. The problems involved are basically the same as those already discussed under Calm Water, though in the case of the awning, the tipped canvas introduced a new problem in perspective: the reflections must tip accordingly.

DRAWING FOG

Did you know that when mist (or smoke) veils the landscape, the thicker the mist, the less the eye can penetrate it. Therefore as objects become more and more distant, they grow progressively less and less distinct until they are entirely enveloped and disappear from view.

The objects that are visible through mist or smoke show no strong contrasts of value. And the greater their distance, the lighter and the flatter they seem to become. Their edges are soft and blurred, scarcely distinguishable in fact.

The little sketch at (3) in Figure 6 gives a simple illustration of this phenomenon. When this drawing was made, powdered graphite (scraped from a pencil) was first rubbed into the paper with a finger. (A pencil stump could also have been used.) Then the pencil was used for the detail, with the artist being sure to keep all objects—particularly those receding into space—light and indefinite.

DRAWING SKIES

Since a light sky is far more brilliant—far lighter—than the whitest drawing paper, you will soon become aware that you can only *suggest* this. In fact you can ignore the exact tone of the sky, simply leaving white paper for all sky areas.

A clear blue sky, no matter how luminous, gives the impression of being darker than a white house, a sail, or some other light object. Cloudy skies vary greatly in tone from the extreme lights of sunlit white clouds to the near-blacks of heavy storm clouds. Skies are so variable that you can safely use them to suit your purpose.

Clouds. Any expert on cloud formations who doesn't realize that the artist is allowed considerable license can be amused at the artist's flaunting of natural laws. In fact you should learn more about clouds than most people usually know, especially if you plan to draw skies above your buildings. (There are numerous sources of information, such as those used by the weather bureau or for aviation.) However, there can be a danger in knowing too much about cloud and other sky effects, unless you learn to control them so that they nicely complement the rest of your subject matter.

Clouds are hard to draw because they move so fast and change shape so often, sometimes even melting away before the eyes. Many artists—particularly in the commercial field—work up some good sky effects (perhaps based on photographs), incorporating them in their drawings when actual sky conditions are not favorable.

(Sky and water, incidentally, must always be consistently related to each other. As you have already learned about reflections, water almost invariably reflects to some extent the sky above, whether clear or cloudy. See Figure 7.)

In drawing clouds you may choose to rely on outline. If so, avoid black, inklike lines (though that will of course depend on the technique you are using in the drawing). Gray lines are usually better. Tone is often superior to even the grayest of lines, with soft, light effects of tone less obtrusive than bolder ones. Medium or fairly hard pencils (used with firm pressure) are generally the best choice, as the granular quality of a soft lead is far from ideal when trying to express clouds or water.

Skies in Architectural Drawings. It is by no means necessary to attempt more than a simple sky treatment in the average architectural drawing. You can leave the sky area untouched altogether, cover it with a uniform tone of gray, or grade it in the simplest manner from dark above to light at the horizon.

The value you select should depend on the tone of the building illustrated. When it's dark or has a dark roof, the sky should be left light, but if light, it is sometimes shown against a dark sky to secure a satisfying contrast, as in (1) of Figure 8. These simple treatments are especially appropriate in rendering formal buildings where many clouds might prove distracting. Picturesque buildings allow greater freedom, since the surroundings should have a character similar to that of the building. But even informal structures may be left with white paper for the sky if there is foliage or other landscape details to add interest to the whole.

In representing a very plain building in a rather monotonous setting, clouds provide the best detail. Even though you may not be able to add trees or other foliage, there is seldom an exterior drawing in which clouds cannot be added if you wish. Nature provides so many kinds and arranges them in so many ways that there is an endless variety from which to choose.

A building of awkward proportion or displeasing contour can be disguised by skillful treatment of the sky. Perspective distortion can also be hidden or made less conspicuous in many cases, while the shadows cast by clouds can be used to great advantage, for instance, if thrown across a monotonous roof or wall surface or upon the ground.

However, clouds, like other accessories, should never be made too prominent. Some students draw the masses so round that the curves fail to harmonize with the straight lines of the architecture. Other students draw such "woolly" strokes or such rough textures that no sense of distance is created—the clouds seeming to be nearer than the architecture itself.

Each line and tone should quietly take its place.

Figure 6. Being able to draw running water, rain, and fog increases your range of landscape skills.

1. Dark sky behind light building

2. Dark sky behind light area of building only

3. Dark sky tone used to throw trees into relief

Figure 8. Skies are important elements for providing contrasts in your drawings.

Unless a drawing is large or done with a very bold, vigorous technique, rather light but firm strokes are best. These should be made with a medium or hard pencil, and you should strive for a silvery gray line, since smoothness suggests distance.

Since skies seem softer in effect and individual clouds smaller in size and less definite as they recede toward the horizon, it is best to have the boldest strokes and the largest and most definite masses near the zenith. Storm clouds, especially those showing strongly contrasting forms and values, are seldom desirable in architectural work, and sunrise or sunset effects detract from the architecture itself, unless they are skillfully handled.

DRAWING SNOW AND ICE

A leading painter known for his landscapes once confessed that, although he had often tried to paint snow scenes, he had never had the slightest success. Certain other painters, on the contrary, have built solid reputations on their portrayals of winter.

To the pen or pencil artist, representing snow should be easy—at least in theory. All you have to do is leave the paper white—or nearly so—wherever snow is to appear, drawing elsewhere only the things not covered with snow. In practice it's not that simple. In fact in one respect the snow painter has it easier than the pen or pencil artist: Just as snow is laid onto the earth in nature, so the painter can brush white (or light) pigment on the canvas. The pen or pencil artist, however, is forced to work in reverse, leaving the paper white or light and fitting all the other tones around the snow areas.

The beginner's most common error is making individual pencil strokes too prominent to accurately represent snow. The natural tones of snow are by no means linear,

so it's hard to interpret them in line. Therefore some of the best representations use tone. This tone is either built up with extreme care—often with a sharp point, which gives it the vibrant quality you want—or rubbed in with the finger or stump of paper.

In Figure 9, for instance, a portion of the snow is "painted" in with a stump of paper that had been rubbed on a blackened sandpaper pad. The lights were then erased with a kneaded eraser. When lines are used, broad strokes of fairly hard pencils, touching or overlapping to minimize their linear quality, are generally best.

Another fault of the beginner is in thinking of snow as pure white in value. In the sunshine snow may be dazzling white, but in shade and shadow it may appear surprisingly dark. Therefore a full gamut of tone may be needed to render it properly. But try it for yourself, either from a photograph or, better yet, from nature.

Ice, whether solid or broken, offers relatively simple problems. There is normally no restless movement required by water in its liquid state. In fact smooth ice makes reflections that are usually indistinct and diffused.

DRAWING CITYSCAPES

Unlike landscape, the impact of the way you draw a cityscape—a street, a square, a small park set against a background of buildings—depends in large part on how you use your pencil, pen, or brush to *relate* different types, sizes, and styles of buildings on the focus you choose, your viewpoint, the direction of light and rather less on more rustic elements such as sky, water, and trees.

In this section, a seemingly simple streetscape made up of a combination of low- and highrise buildings is developed step by step into a powerful drawing.

Figure 9. A stump of paper was used here to "draw in" the snow.

EXERCISE 4: CITYSCAPES

In all cityscapes perspective must be closely observed, which makes accuracy in the lay-in drawing very important. Even though you don't have to make actual vanishing points, you must be very aware of all perspective lines at eye level. Since you want to show the effect of height, for instance, use a low eye level. Indicate all the major branches on the tree, keeping it light against dark and middle tones.

After you lay in the drawing with a 4H pencil, indicate tall background buildings with a 6H pencil. Do not press hard so you can obtain a slight variation in tone. Before you finish the light area, put in the dark areas on the left side with a 2B pencil. Make sure there is enough separation between the dark value and the light buildings in the background.

Put in all the shadow areas of the houses and finish the building on the left with a 2B pencil. With a 2H pencil draw in the foreground area and the shadows under the eaves. By rendering only the dark areas, you can see the value pattern of the drawing. The small darks on the right balance the larger dark building on the left.

Starting with the houses on the right, put in the middle tone with a 2H pencil. The light is coming from the left, so you want these houses to become lighter in value as they reach the large dark mass on the left. With the values darker on the right, you can also make the tree stand out. The windows are indicated with an HB pencil and the steps and car with a 4H pencil.

To complete the front of the houses, use a 4H pencil. Indicate the tree using very little modeling with a 4H pencil. Finish the drawing with an HB pencil by placing small accents in the windows, railing, doors, TV antenna, and tree.

EXAMPLES

These examples of sketching and rendering of architectural landscape, in cities and in the country, show a varied range of techniques important artists and designers have used to capture character.

HANDLING LARGE LANDSCAPES: ROBERT LOCKWOOD

GENEROUS USE OF TONE: RICHARD POWERS

In this Richard Powers pen and ink drawing, tone has
been applied to virtually all the wall and roof surfaces, as
well as to broad but selected parts of the landscaping,
which gets more than the usual attention from the artist.
In the detail of the full-scale reproduction, note the
"hooked" effect of many lines used to define the bark of
the larger tree.

(Pages 140–141) In this grand landscape, Robert
Lockwood leads the viewer's eye gradually back from the
foreground to the distant buildings. Yet each detail in
this pen and ink drawing is carefully delineated, without
losing the free and open feeling of the whole. Note the
special pattern created by the foreground.

USING SOFT PENCIL TO TEST IDEAS: MARK SIMON

In this drawing for the Bellamy-Simon house at Stony Creek, Connecticut, Mark Simon used soft pencil on vellum yellow tracing paper to capture the style of the house and the mood of the landscaping. The drawing, 11″ × 8½″ (28 × 22 cm), is one stage in Simon's method of rapid, progressive changes as his sketches keep pace with his ideas. The pencil is dark, so it can be seen through several layers of tracing paper, and it is also easy to erase, giving the designer added freedom.

TYING A BUILDING TO ITS SITE: BERTRAM GROSVENOR GOODHUE

In this drawing of black crayon on paper of an unbuilt house in Westchester County, New York, Bertram Grosvenor Goodhue locks the house into the hill by extending the walls of the building down the side of the slope. The blank walls are accented only by the neo-Gothic detailing and the use of small bays and towers. The 40″ × 27″ (102 × 69 cm) drawing was made in 1915.

Courtesy Collection of John Rivers, Houston, Texas.

CONVEYING A SENSE OF PLACE: CHARLES MOORE

It is the architect's responsibility, says Charles Moore, to create a sense of place "in space, time and the order of things." Through the architect's work one should be better able "to perceive and assimilate the delights and complexities of an untheoretical world." An application of that philosophy can be seen in this first scheme for the University of California Faculty Club at Santa Barbara. Drawn 11″ × 14″ (28 × 36 cm) in pencil on vellum, this 1969 perspective recalls the massing of vernacular buildings, in what has become known as the "Bay Area tradition."

Courtesy Architectural Archives, University of California, Santa Barbara.

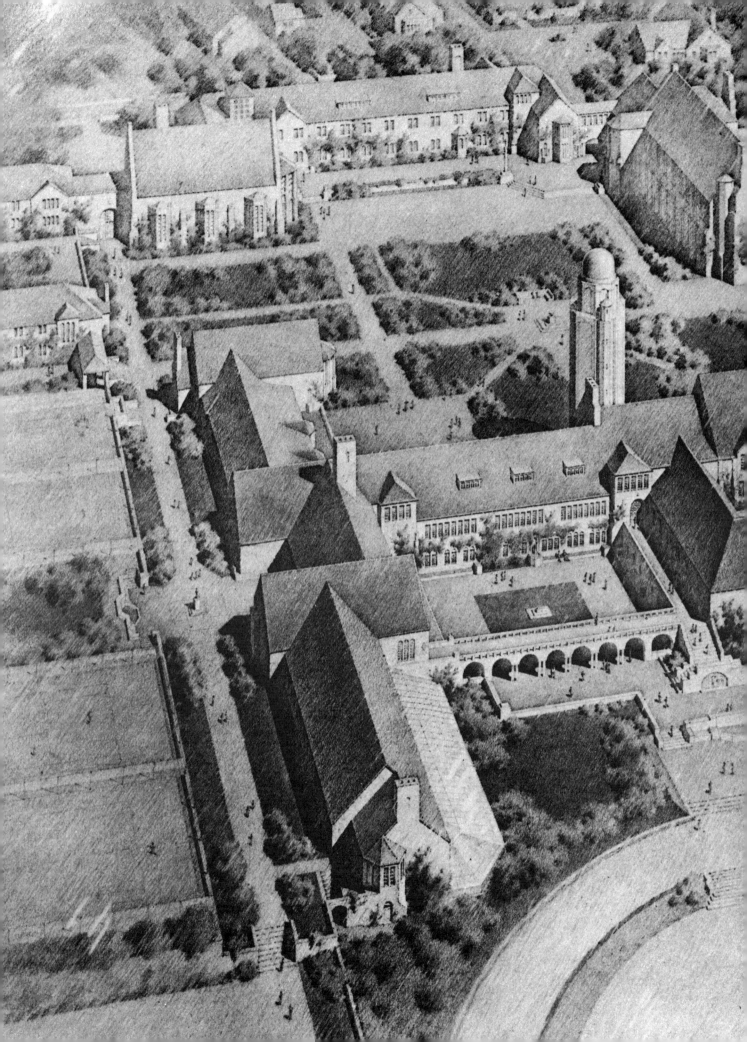

BIRD'S-EYE VIEWS: ELIEL SAARINEN AND WALTER BURLEY GRIFFIN

In this 1926 bird's eye view of the Cranbrook School in Bloomfield Hills, Michigan, Eliel Saarinen created a vision of the educational environment that he would help build over the next twenty years. It was his belief, shared with the founders of the German Bauhaus, that in such a community the fine arts and crafts should be integrated with the technology of the twentieth century. There mature artists could work and students could come to study with them. Saarinen's design, drawn here 21½″ × 25⅝″ (55 × 65 cm) in graphite on illustration board, is an abstraction of medieval forms stripped of intricate, nostalgic detailing.

Courtesy Cranbrook Academy of Art Museum, Bloomfield Hills, Michigan.

(Overleaf) As a member of Frank Lloyd Wright's Prairie School movement, which advocated building with nature, Walter Burley Griffin is known for his sensitive and imaginative approach to landscaping. Shown here is his project for Trier Center Neighborhood in Winnetka, Illinois, conceived in 1912–13. The plan, which was drawn in ink on linen 21″ × 31″ (53 × 79 cm), is noted for its emphasis on plants, shrubs, and trees, since Griffin's intent was to preserve as rural an environment as possible in this housing subdivision.

Courtesy the Burnham Library, the Art Institute of Chicago, Chicago, Illinois.

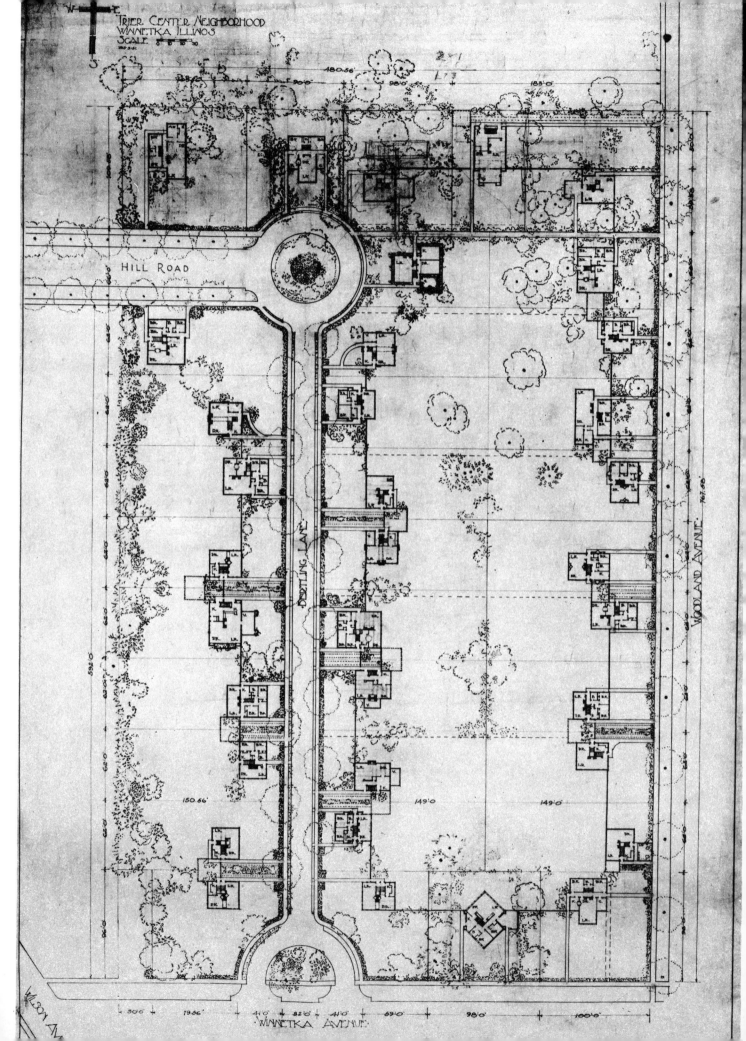

TRIER CENTER NEIGHBORHOOD
WINNETKA ILLINOIS
SCALE

HILL ROAD

DRIELING LANE

WOODLAND AVENUE

WINNETKA AVENUE

WILSON AV

CHAPTER NINE
DRAWING FROM PHOTOGRAPHS

Herbert S. Kates

In theory it's not desirable to draw from photographs. Even granting the claim that the camera cannot lie, photographs are often full of apparent distortions of mass and errors in value. When practical, it is much better to go to natural sources for subjects. There you can not only study each subject from various points of view, noting such things as mass, light and shade, color and texture, but you can also get the "feel" of the entire surroundings and interpret the essentials in your own way.

In practice, however, the average student, especially at first, is helplessly lost. If you pick a building or street scene, for instance, you see such a bewildering quantity of things that it's hard to know where to begin. You don't know how much to include, how to show the proper perspective, how to suggest some texture, or how to represent tones of color in light and shade. Just when you finally think you've solved some problems, the light has changed, producing entirely different effects of color and altering patterns of shade and shadow. This chapter therefore shows you how to use photographs to help you make better drawings.

SOME PRACTICAL SUGGESTIONS

Making a few drawings from photographs helps you prepare for later work from nature. There are also times when the experienced artist is forced to work from photographs for a variety of reasons. Here are some practical suggestions on how to use them to fullest advantage.

Drawing from photographs is comparatively easy, especially when black and white prints eliminate the distractions of color. Light and shade are fixed, so they can be used at any time of day and placed in any relationship to the artist. Also the artist doesn't have to fear the interruptions of curious passersby.

Photographs represent subjects in a conveniently simplified manner. They do contain distortions, however, often in the corners or any areas outside the range normally viewed by the human eye. They also fail to represent values accurately. Shadow tones in particular are seldom shown with sufficient transparency; portions that in the original could be readily discerned by the eye often appear black or nearly so.

Selecting the Photograph. Take all these things into account in drawing from photographs. First make sure you have a good print, rejecting any that shows marked distortions or unnatural effects. Try to find subjects that are well composed. If not, you may have to recompose or make such changes as lightening tones that are too dark or darkening those that

appear too light, correcting unnatural perspective or distorted shapes, and frequently omitting nonessential features—all of which takes extra time and skill.

It's easiest to get interesting results if each photograph you select has a focal point or center of interest. This might be an archway or doorway in a building. Be sure there is not a rival point, although there can be one or more subordinate centers of lesser interest.

Study the Values. Begin by blocking out the subject carefully in pencil outline on the final paper. While doing this freehand work, it's important that you place the photo in plain sight and be sure it's not tipped, for unless your eye is looking at right angles to its surface, it will appear foreshortened and you will draw incorrect proportions in your sketch. For the same reason hold your paper in the proper position. If the photograph is small, try drawing a bit larger. Don't lay out a subject so tiny that it demands finicky pen work.

When you have completely blocked out the subject, make a thorough analysis of the values, comparing and studying them to see which you can eliminate or simplify. It may be easier to compare values if you lay extremely thin tracing paper over the photograph through which the values will show in simplified form. Are some too dark or light to look natural? Are all essential or can some be eliminated?

Take a soft pencil and make a quick sketch of the basics, tracing important outlines and toning in the significant values. The tracing, touched up a bit, stands ready to serve as a guide for your pen work.

As you make this tracing, think of the direction from which the light is falling, of the source from which it comes, and of the shade and shadows that naturally result. (Remember that shadows frequently offer some of the most important dark values.) Then too note the textures and tones of the various materials. In deciding what

areas are to be left white and what made dark, keep this in mind: If there is to be one principal light area and one leading dark area (a scheme both common and desirable), select them immediately.

Working with Pencil or Pen. It is best to start at the center of interest and work out from there, continuing the sketch only until the drawing includes enough area and is sufficiently rendered to properly convey its message. The knowledge of where to stop and when to stop and how to stop comes only with practice; the preliminary sketch will help in all three respects.

There are very few hints for mak-

ing the sketch itself, for each subject demands its own peculiar treatment and every artist soon finds a favorite method. The size and kind of pen, brush, or pencil you use will be governed mainly by the size of the drawing and the type of subject.

Don't think too much about technique. There is and should be no set rule. Represent everything, whether color, tone, or texture, in what seems to you a logical way. Usually something about each part of the subject will suggest both the character and direction of line. If in doubt refer to drawings of similar subjects by other artists; compare their methods and then do the things in the way that appeals to you. In any case don't

Figure 1. This is an old photograph of Arco della Conca in Perugia, Italy, on which this demonstration is based.

allow the technique to become so conspicuous that it detracts from the subject itself.

A SIMPLE DEMONSTRATION

The photograph in Figure 1 is of the Arco della Conca in Perugia, Italy. This photo is well composed, with the interest centered in the arched doorway at the convergence of the street lines, which help lead the eye to it. The doorway itself and the adjacent dark window openings form strong accents that help focus attention on the central group of buildings. Attention is also directed to this point by the large archway, with its dark intrados tone, which serves as a frame for the whole composition.

In this photograph the values of light and shade are well disposed and natural, with the exception of the principal dark of the large arch, which is too black. The shadow tones form an interesting composition or pattern; there is a pleasing variety of textures in the materials. Therefore it seemed reasonable to carry out the same general scheme of composition in the drawing.

In Figure 2 the values generally have been kept lighter and more transparent, and the white paper takes the place of the lighter gray tones. The dark mass on the right has been made lighter and the vegetation above the larger arch, which seems somewhat too prominent, is brought

out less distinctly. The entire left portion has also been simplified.

While no slavish attempt has been made to copy much detail, a type of line has been chosen that suggests the rough textures of the old materials. No absolutely straight lines have been drawn; many of the lines are hooked on the ends, and in some places, notably the dark intrados tone of the large arch, crosshatch has been used.

This drawing has been vignetted toward the edges, and these vary greatly in handling. While it is easy to build up the values near the center of interest, one of the hardest things to do is to blend the drawing into the paper in an interesting manner at the

Figure 2. This is the drawing that was made from Figure 1. Here the entire photograph was used for reference.

Figure 3. Harvey Ellis made an altogether different drawing—in terms of technique and value placement—of the same scene.

Figure 4. You can crop Figure 1 in many ways. Here are several possible variations composed from the same photograph.

edges. The silhouette or pattern that an entire drawing makes against the paper is most important.

A street scene like this often looks barren and deserted when there are no people. The photo shows several figures almost lost in the tones toward the left; so nearly lost that they were omitted from the drawing. A figure or two in the foreground toward the right, catching the light and contrasting with the dark behind them, or placed beneath the arch and drawn almost in black, would add much interest to the drawing, particularly because of the large area of rather tiresome gray toward the right.

When in doubt about something like this, put tracing paper over your drawing and experiment. Better yet, sketch the figures to the proper scale on another sheet of paper, cut them out, and try them in different positions on the drawing, later adding the corrections to the finished work. In many photos people are standing self-consciously facing the camera. Be sure to draw them in more natural positions.

Look at the drawing of the same subject by Harvey Ellis in Figure 3. This drawing was probably done on the site from nearly the same viewpoint. Ellis treated the subject with fewer lines and greater freedom. The angle of the light rays was also different, so the shadow masses were not the same shape. The most interesting difference, however, is the way in which he reversed the values of the viaduct and the sky—the former left rather light and the latter made dark.

The reversal in this case probably has no significance. Often, however, the artist deliberately reverses the values he or she finds in nature if it serves a purpose to do so. For example, if the roof of a building were actually light against a dark blue sky, the artist may decide to let the white paper represent the sky and may darken the roof instead to gain the needed contrast. There is often an advantage in reversing nature's scheme, provided that you do so intelligently.

Note several possible ways of cropping the photograph shown in Figure 4.

EXERCISE 1: ST. GEORGE TUCKER HOUSE

Don't bother changing the house itself. The angles of the roofs and chimneys are so interesting that you can leave them as they are. The foreground and the background, however, should be changed considerably. Simplify the trees in the background, since you don't want them to become too dominant. In order to have a place for the eye to move into the picture (and also because the fence creates too much of a barrier), open a gate in the fence. Since more dark tones are on the left, bring more interest to the right by moving the small building to that area.

EXERCISE 2: THE GOVERNOR'S PALACE

Very few changes need to be made to do this drawing. Move the main tree away from the left post of the gate because it creates too much of a straight line. Also omit the posts and chains in front of the palace gates. And don't clutter the foreground with additional spots. The road is strong enough an element to move the viewer's eye to the gate where it should be focused. Don't draw the dark branches and leaves as a frame for the upper part of the drawing. It will add a distracting area and take attention away from the gates.

Maybe you should include a few figures in the foreground. Although the artist left them out for the same reason he excluded the fence, it could add an interesting touch.

Hugh Ferriss's charcoal pencil technique captures the monumentality of the imaginary skyscraper in this bird's-eye view showing the huge building's ties to the roadway below. Three levels of tone are used to vary the emphasis from skyscraper shaft (dark), to adjacent structures (medium), to background (light).

PART THREE
PERSONAL APPROACHES

The great artists of pen and pencil came to fame in part—or perhaps especially—because they perfected a personal style. The style at times depended on a unique way in which they manipulated their medium—thick slabs of flat pencil, finely detailed areas of thin ink strokes, a fresh combination of bold, irregular lines. Or else their choice of subject matter—tranquil domestic buildings in broad landscapes, strong renderings of massive buildings, the hubbub of street life—serves as a signature to their work. Often, the approach to their subject matter sets them apart: The appeal rests on a romantic flair, a classical balance, or a fine sense of whimsy. And it is these moods that set one artist or designer apart from another.

You will find that the three artists whose work is shown in this section differ sharply in their approach to subject matter and in the way they use their tools. Norman Diekman's drawings of interiors are calm and ordered. The sketches of Paul Hogarth are light and humorous, almost cartoons. Hugh Ferriss's buildings, dams, and factories give a sense of power and drama. Compare their styles and decide which, if any, fits your own approach to drawing.

CHAPTER TEN

CREATING ORDER WITH DRAWING: NORMAN DIEKMAN

Norman Diekman uses drawings to help him design a project. The project shown in this chapter is a one-bedroom apartment in an existing building, and this study shows the ways in which refinement of detail can make something special from an ordinary space. The drawings are in no way theoretical, but immediate means to an urgently needed reality.

The project was completed in 1982, and the drawings reflect the type of work most often done in Diekman's studio. Generally, his design process is as follows: Initial concept sketches are made with Pentel pens, charcoal pencils, and/or Prismacolor pencils in sketch books or on whatever paper is at hand. Once the concept drawings look interesting, scaled drawings are developed. These are usually drawn in scale on 18″ or 24″ (46- or 61-cm) cream tracing paper with a combination of soft lead pencils, marker ink on the back of the drawing for general tone, and Prismacolor pencil on the face of the drawing for gradation, shading, and surface texture.

All developed drawings are laid out, refined, and corrected on an undersheet (the base sheet) before tracing presentation drawings are made on a cream overlay. The drawings that show white areas on the face of the paper require special care and skill in execution because the soft graphite pencil smudges and smears easily into the white. Because of this, the technique is usually reserved for fully rendered presentation drawings.

HOW THE PROJECT EVOLVED

The space illustrated here is a one-bedroom apartment in a modern (post-war, 1950s or 1960s) highrise building of the sort of nondescript character commonplace in almost any large city. Views from the windows are not extraordinary, although the quality of light from the windows is an attractive feature.

The clients, a business couple, have some special requirements. The living space is to be treated more as a studio than a conventional living room—a space where an art collection can be studied and worked over and where some creative work, at modest scale, can also be done. Books are a major interest; some 3,000 are to be accommodated, calling for 27 linear feet (8 m) of shelving in 3′ (1 m) wide, 8′ (2 m) high units. There is a small collection of art objects to be displayed, and the main living-studio area must serve for occasional entertainment in some style.

Out of these realities, certain thematic ideas develop. The cramped access to kitchen, closets, bedroom, and bath is a problem requiring some special attention. The studio function of the main living area suggests a second theme relating to the idea of a large movable table that will dominate this part of the space. The need to provide for the large collection of books becomes a third theme. Ways of dealing with these three issues became the essence of the project.

An early concept proposal focuses

on kitchen, bath, and closet areas. A storage core is projected into the living space as a way of resolving the confusion where all the spaces converge. This scheme calls for a major construction effort, which will involve inevitable major costs. A second design study centers on a sliding door or grille that will clarify the spatial relationships between core and living-studio areas.

One of the major assets of the existing space is the flux of light—light of special and beautiful quality. This leads to a search for ways to preserve awareness of this light penetration while still sorting out space relationships. This concern leads to the idea of a grille door, by which to articulate space, but not cut off flow and visibility of light.

Once this idea has surfaced, studies turn to an exploration of grilles—grilles with hinged door portions and grilles that can relate to book storage. First, the use of standard steel book shelving was investigated, and then the possibilities for special treatment of the door to the kitchen.

A split kitchen door was developed to let light through while cutting off direct view into the kitchen. Attention is thus shifting more and more from a study of objects to a concern for the impact of light and patterns of vision. The idea of a quiet, soft space suffused with a light that could also be described as quiet and soft emerges as the concept that dominates this project.

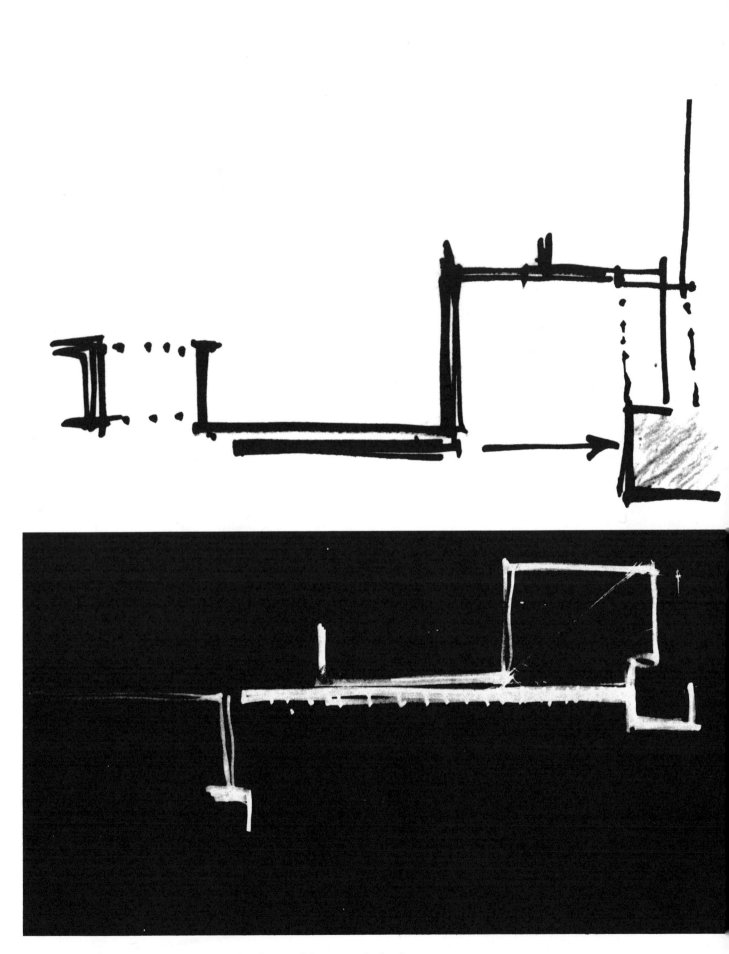

*Two quick pen drawings illustrate the dividing wall between the kitchen/
bathroom core area and the main living space.*

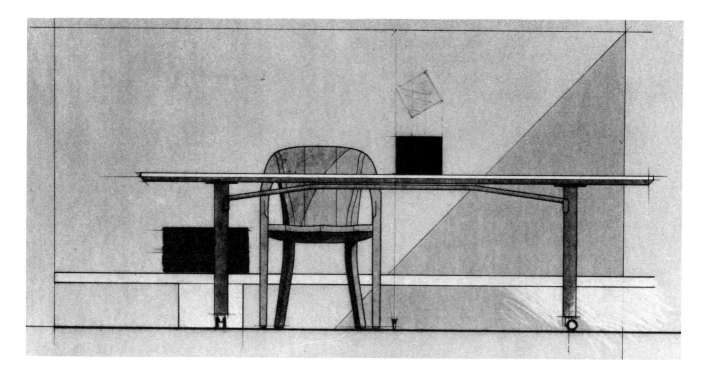

The large table that is to be the focus of the main living space is now developed in relation to the grille wall. This table is always placed at a slight angle to the main axes of the room, an angle that implies mobility. The table is indeed intended to be mobile as its big caster wheels suggest, but its mobility is also an idea going beyond the actual reality. The dividing wall with its grille pattern remains the central theme of the space and connects with the treatment of the shelving in the bedroom space beyond. This is a simple grid of square box spaces in white-lacquered wood—a grid or grille in larger scale containing storage and whatever other objects and elements are to appear in this room.

The island book storage unit at the left of the main living space is functionally useful, but also acts as a foil in relation to the grille-storage wall next to it. A modest bench, intended for stacking, displaying, and studying books, is added to complete the relationship of elements making up a simple, but still subtle and complex space.

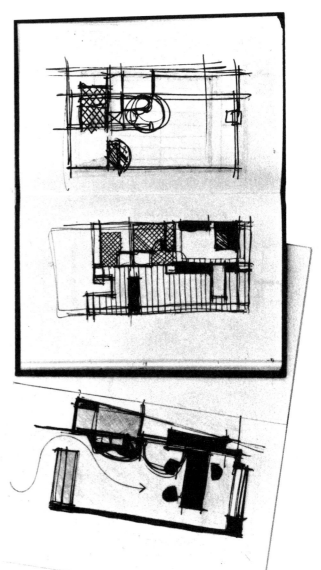

A study (above) concerns subtleties of proportion in the relationship of living room furniture elements—table, bench, and chair.

Two sketchbooks (right) contain plan development studies.

Here are the bath-storage core areas (opposite page). Note visible scale and section AA locating line. This remains a design study although the level of detail considered is quite precise. A fully rendered perspective of section AA is shown below.

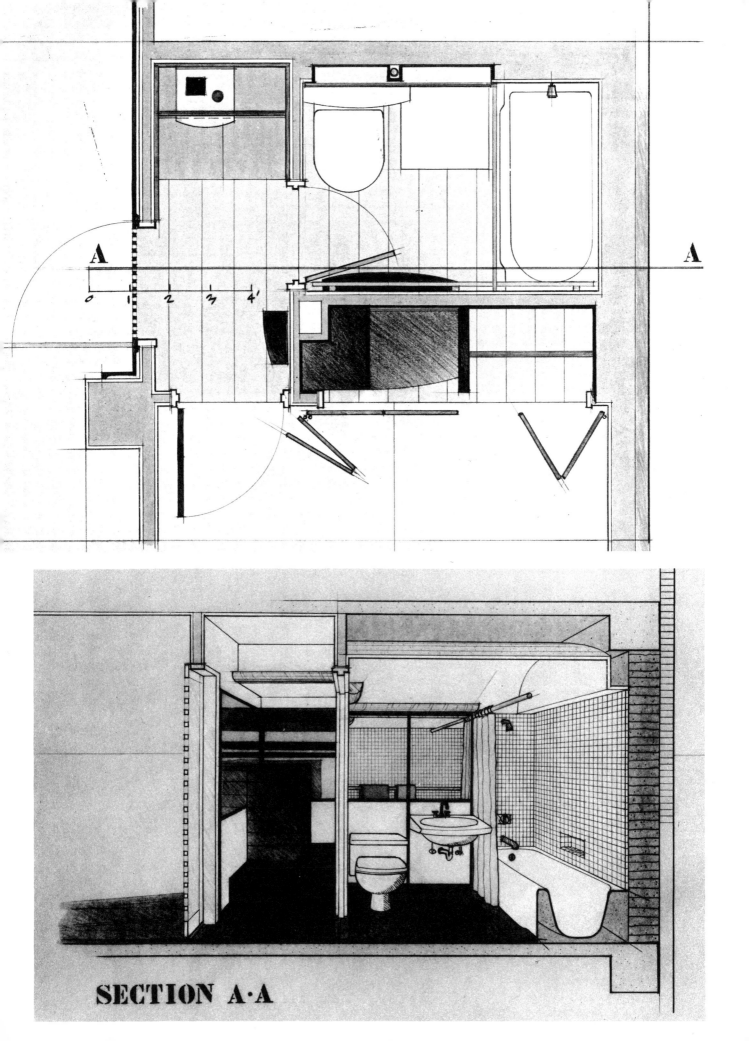

A · A

SECTION A · A

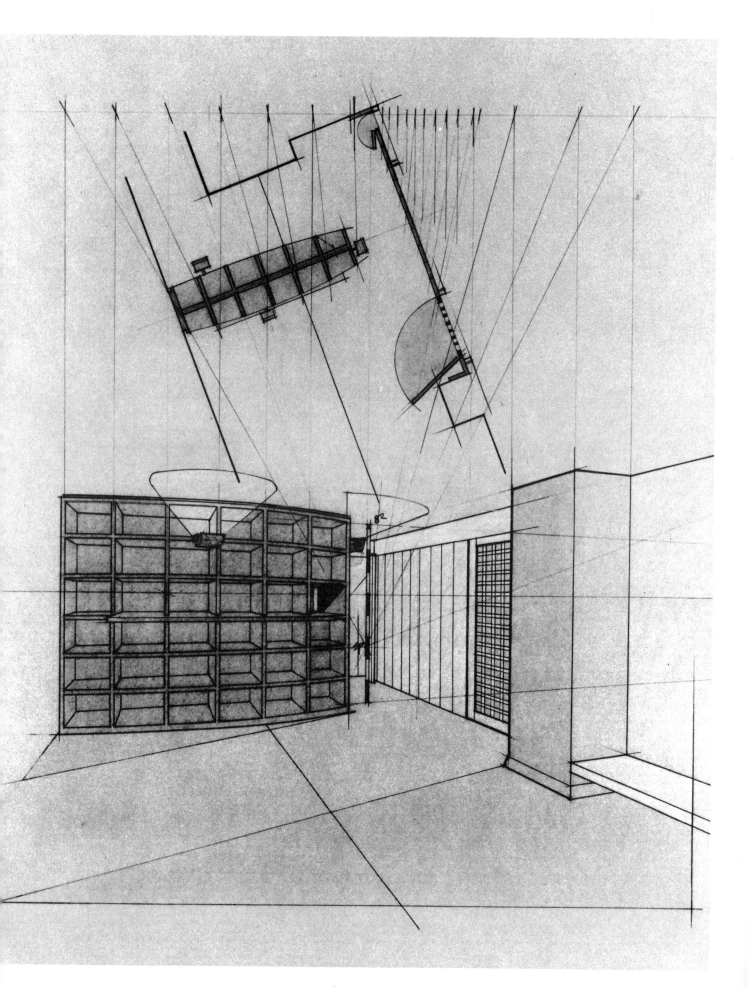

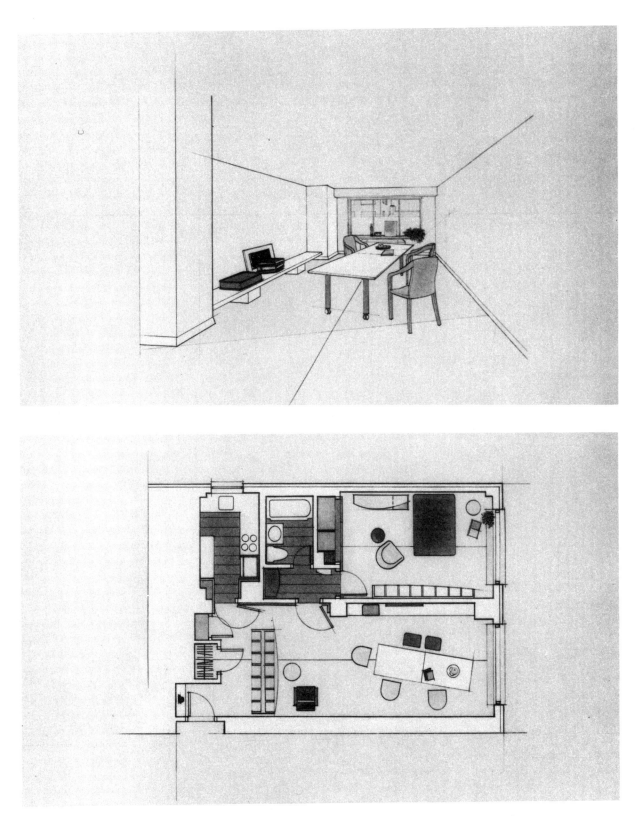

A final design study of table and bench area (top) is shown in perspective. Note that construction lines (bottom) are visible in the final drawing, giving a hint of its studio origins.

A studio working layout (opposite page) has the final form of grille, dividing wall, and bookcase shown in perspective projection.

*A drawing for final presentation shows bedroom area with fabric,
color, and materials plus the grid bookcase superimposed.*

CHAPTER ELEVEN
THE ART OF CARICATURE: PAUL HOGARTH

From the Preface and Introduction to Paul Hogarth's *Drawing Architecture* from which the following drawings were selected.

In his book Drawing Architecture: A Creative Approach, *Paul Hogarth passes on to us some of the wisdom—sharpened by his world travels—that he has acquired, and illustrates it with drawings that positively crackle with wit and athletic observation. . . .*

. . . like every good artist, he knows that architecture is more than buildings, however grand, famous, or intricate they may be. It is also the small things that matter: paving stones and trash cans; lettering and manhole covers; beggars and policemen; and mail boxes and shoes. All these things together with light, texture, smells, and movement make one place different from another. Only by noting and then drawing all these architectural variables will the artist recognize, love, and fully understand architecture.

Sir Hugh Casson

Drawing buildings of any period (classical or commercial vernacular) becomes a matter of personal interpretation. And so I have always regarded it as one of the most adventurous and spirited areas of my work. . . .

My interest in architecture preceded any idea of how I would actually draw a building. There was no one around who might have ended my dilemma by saying "why don't you think of them as monsters or even odd-shaped people?" Such a suggestion would have enabled me to see buildings as entities and shapes, and not as vast, anonymous piles of masonry that had to be faithfully rendered with an HB graphite pencil. I also had to evolve my own subject selection. It took a great deal of time, wandering, and self-study before I could draw architecture the way I wanted.

After a series of false starts, I began to move toward a breakthrough. During 1953–54, I went on a series of travels in war-shattered Europe and Asia. Historical architecture began to qualify as a subject for my pencil, and I sat before the fine old palaces and cathedrals of Czechoslovakia, Germany, Poland, and Italy

mourning their loss or celebrating their reconstruction. In China, I witnessed the dramatic building of large-scale industrial architecture which was to proclaim an immense social revolution.

Of course, more often than not, I failed in my attempts, but one satisfaction kept me at it; the more I tackled the buildings that aroused my sense of history, the more confidence I acquired. I discovered, too, that after I began my explorations into the potentials of different media, I found that very often a repertoire of pencils, inks, markers, and watercolor might well be the key to depicting more complex subjects. My drawing became more essentially architectural; the emphasis on either line, structure, or monumentality produced a generally expressive effect of rhythmic order laced with occasional fantasy. . . .

Sometimes the power of a drawing is found not so much in its faithfulness to the subject but in its revelation of something you did not know or understand before. I hope you will find, as I have, that drawing architecture can give you a nostalgia for the past, as well as a greater awareness of the present.

St. Mary Panachrantos, Istanbul, Turkey, 1966. This is one of a series of historical illustrations depicting life in the twelfth-century Constantinople that Hogarth made for Time-Life books. The church is intact and in remarkably good shape despite its great age. Byzantine architects lavished a great deal of attention on interior spaces and mosaics. Outside decorations were left to imaginative masons who spaced out stone with friezes and rosettes of brick imbedded in colored mortar.

To convey something of these textural effects, Hogarth first blocked out the shape of the church with a large Japanese brush charged with washes of diluted Pelikan permanent black writing ink. Then he painted the decorative masonry with Winsor & Newton No. 4 and No. 6 sable brushes in undiluted Higgins India ink. He used Daler drawing paper as a surface and a Gillot 303 nib to delineate the barred windows. (From Byzantium, a volume in The Great Age of Man series, Time-Life Books. © 1966, Time, Inc., New York.)

Dresden, Germany, 1960 (left). By working with different angles of light—the sun in front or behind—and by using different drawing media, mood and atmosphere can be created. This helps express the character of architecture. For example, this ruined baroque church in Dresden was drawn against the afternoon sun with a soft Hardtmuth charcoal lead and a harder Conté Pierre Noir lead for the pedimented frontage in the right foreground. In this way Hogarth was able to express more graphically the essential nobility of the classical style. (From Hogarth's private collection of unpublished drawings.)

The Congregational Church, Windsor, Connecticut. On the other hand, this church (right) was drawn with the sun behind Hogarth. He used Spencerian and Gillot 303 nibs for the linear work and a Japanese brush to fill in the solid areas. He was thus able to convey the church's puritanical severity extremely effectively. (Reproduced by permission of the owner, Tom Mathews, Cavendish, England.)

LOVELL

SMITH

BELL

BAILEY
WILLIAM BAILEY
1844-1928

WRISLEY

PLUMB
ANDREW WILLIAM PLUMB
1853-1913
MARY ELLA HOWARD
HIS WIFE
1876-1939

SETH STRONG
CO E 14 REGT
ARTY. R.I. VOL
DIED
MAR 1 1885

CIVIL WAR
CHARLES DANIELS
Co.A 1st C.V.H.A.
DIED MAR 16 1916
Æ 85

Broadway at Times Square, New York, 1963 (above). Concentrating on a focal point, leaving out unnecessary detail, and drawing only what is strictly essential invariably increase the pace and tension of a big city subject. Hogarth drew this in an hour with a Gillot 303 nib and Higgins India ink on white Saunders paper. (Originally reproduced on the jacket of Brendan Behan's New York, 1964. Courtesy Hutchinson Publishing Group, London; and Bernard Geis Associates, New York.)

Street Scene, Staten Island, New York, 1963 (right). The older suburbs with ornate wooden frame houses dating from the 1890s are goldmines of hauntingly nostalgic material. Hogarth drew this house with a Spencerian school nib, a Japanese brush, and Higgins India ink on Saunders paper. (From Brendan Behan's New York, 1964. Courtesy Hutchinson Publishing Group, London; and Bernard Geis Associates, New York. Reproduced by permission of the owner, Christopher Walker of Cambridge, England.)

Street scene on STATEN ISLAND

Springfield, Massachusetts, 1963 (left). Here Hogarth wanted to place industrial architecture—the Westinghouse plant—in a suburban setting. However, as he drove through the suburb, he found the vintage frame houses all scattered and unrelated to each other, as well as to the plant. So he created a composite drawing by selecting various elements from different locations and combining them into one drawing. This study was drawn on Saunders paper in Higgins India ink and Grumbacher watercolors. (Courtesy Fortune *magazine. © December 1963 by Time, Inc., New York.)*

Old Pratt Read Plant, Ivoryton, Connecticut, 1963 (right). Hogarth took a while to define this building with its vast area of brickwork. Old industrial buildings often have finely crafted detail; to capture this is to convey the essence of a Victorian plant. This was drawn with a Gillot 303 nib, a Spencerian school nib, and Higgins India ink on Saunders paper. The solid areas were filled in with a Japanese brush and then blotted. (Courtesy Fortune *magazine. © December 1963 by Time, Inc., New York. Reproduced by permission of the owner, Library of Congress, Washington, D.C.)*

CHAPTER TWELVE
POWER AND DRAMA: HUGH FERRISS

From the Foreword and Introduction to *Architectural Visions* by Jean Ferriss Leich from which the following drawings were selected.

As if all the hidden drama of his drawings wanted out in words too, there comes a point, almost suddenly, when Ferriss breaks into pure poetry.

Buildings like crystals
Walls of translucent glass
Sheer glass blocks sheathing
*   a steel grill*
No Gothic branch: no Acanthus leaf:
*   no recollection of the plant world*
A mineral kingdom
Gleaming stalagmites
Forms as cold as ice
Mathematics
Night in the Science Zone

This could have been written by a German Expressionist or a Russian Constructivist after 1917, a Bruno Taut, or a Tatlin. It is another facet of Hugh Ferriss's truly modern sensibility—a sensibility which once again shines through the following pages with undiminished vigor and magic.

Adolf K. Placzek

Although often described as an "illustrator," the word may be applied to Ferriss only if one recalls that he was an illustrator not so much of buildings as of momumental forms and their relationships in space. Mountains and pyramids, dams and skyscrapers, all struck a responsive chord in him, and in drawing them he was primarily concerned with basic structure and mass. The essentially abstract nature of his work is most evident, perhaps, in renderings of imaginary subjects, but it is true as well of all his best drawings of actual buildings, in which surface detail is modified, or even discarded altogether. Although his technique has been decried, on occasion, as "blurred" and "ambiguous" (on the assumption that it sprang from a desire to mask or distort architectural reality), Ferriss himself maintained that his intention was to expose, not suppress, the truth of the building as he saw it: ". . . the underlying truth of a building is that it is a Mass in Space. . . . I usually, as a first step, put down some light lines or tones which suggest (to me, as I am drawing) the existence of the three dimensions of Space. By gradually increasing the definition of these lines . . . I produce, to my own mind, the illusion of forming Mass within this Space. . . . In general, I fancy the finished result as emerging gradually, and as a whole, from the background."

The greatest accuracy in the world, Ferriss argued, will not in itself convey the complex impression that a building makes upon the eye and mind of the beholder: The truthful rendering must be a synthesis not only of structural, but of emotional and intellectual facts. The draftsman must consider his subject as an assemblage of structural parts, resting firmly on the ground, but this is only the beginning of his task. The atmosphere that modifies the building should be suggested as well, in texture and color, in light and shade.

Another demanding aspect of the delineator's art is implying in a single, fixed image the composite impression received by the passerby. Viewed in this way, any building is an object in motion. All this, however, is a prelude to the renderer's most important aim: portraying the psychological content of the subject. Buildings, Ferriss said, "possess an individual existence . . . now dynamic, now serene," and it is the duty of the delineator, as of any conscientious portraitist, to be alert to the "emotional tone, the particular mood" of his subject. In such "outlying psychological domains," rendering "like the other arts, may attain its happiest freedom of movement. . . ."

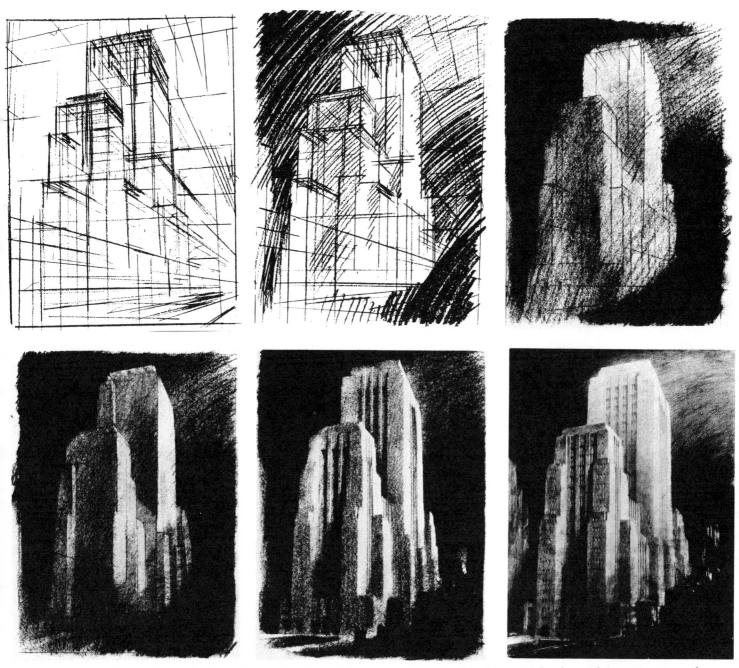

Progressive Views of a Rendering. (From a Ferriss article on architectural rendering that appeared in Encyclopedia Britannica from 1929 to 1961.) From left to right and top down, Ferriss first drew lines, suggesting the mass of the building, followed by more lines as he began to develop tone, using a 3B crayon. Next, he used a paper stump or gloved finger to rub lines together, yielding added tonal values to bring out the building mass. Ferriss then began to develop a three-tier system of tones—dark for the background, medium for surfaces facing to the left, and lightest for those facing to the right. In the fifth drawing, the previous procedure of crayon, paper stump, and kneeded eraser was repeated, and a fourth tone was added for shadow. This procedure was repeated, working with smaller parts of the drawing, until the final effect stood out.

Perisphere and Trylon during construction at 1939–1940 New York World's Fair. This charcoal and charcoal pencil drawing on buff paper successfully captured the twin theme image of the fair: the round structure of the earth and the vertical unit pointing to tomorrow. The original of this 19½" × 15" (50 × 38 cm) drawing is owned by Christopher Leich, Ferriss's grandson.

(Overleaf) National Airport, Washington, D.C., 1941. This drawing, 24½" × 19½" (62 × 50 cm), done in charcoal and charcoal pencil on Bristol board, aims at recording an impression received at the actual building site. It is drawn as though seen at night, as indeed it was. Artificial light was coming from within the building and was reflected from planes on the apron. The moon is visible, looming large above the arrow of the floodlit Washington Monument. The aim here was to show the building as it looked to actual people, not on the drafting board. Commissioned by the Public Buildings Administration, Howard L. Cheney was the consulting architect while Louis A. Simon was the supervising architect.

Lever House, New York, 1952. The drawing captures the sleekness and shimmer of this skyscraper, among the first glass and metal curtain wall office buildings that was to spread across the country in the next thirty years. Using charcoal and charcoal pencil on board, Ferriss also sought to focus on the opened-up ground floor, made possible by a provision of the New York City zoning law that gave builders a height premium in return for having a building take up 25 percent or less of the site. A light source emanating from within the first floor enclosure is allowed to spill out across the open plaza areas and the Park Avenue sidewalk in the foreground. The drawing is quite small—10³⁄₁₆" × 10⁵⁄₁₆" (26 × 27 cm). The architects were Skidmore, Owings and Merrill.

Proposed Alterations, Metropolitan Museum of Art, New York, 1946. In 1946, Metropolitan Museum of Art and New York City officials launched a drive for large-scale alterations and additions to mark the Museum's 75th anniversary. This charcoal pencil on tracing paper sketch 18" × 17" (46 × 43 cm), was done to show that even in the older and more familiar portions of the building, many stone moldings and projections, once seen as essential, were earmarked for removal, to echo the trend toward a simplified architecture. Note that Ferriss used a dark tone to frame the lighter tone of the vaulted entrance lobby. Robert B. O'Connor and Aymar Embury II were the architects.

Norris Dam, Tennessee, 1936. With subtle variations of a medium tone, Ferriss captures the great mass and grand sweep of this huge concrete structure, underscored by the small scale figure in the foreground. Charcoal and charcoal pencil on heavy board were used on this 22″ × 15″ (56 × 38 cm) drawing. Architects and engineers of the Tennessee Valley Authority were responsible for this monumental structure.

CREDITS

The material for this book has been drawn from the following Whitney Library of Design and Watson-Guptill titles.

SELECTED BIBLIOGRAPHY

The following works served as the basis for this book.

Allen, Gerald, and Richard Oliver. *Architectural Drawing: The Art and the Process*. New York: Whitney Library of Design, 1981.

Borgman, Harry. *Drawing in Ink*. New York: Watson-Guptill Publications, 1977.

————. *Drawing in Pencil*. New York: Watson-Guptill Publications, 1981.

Diekman, Norman, and John Pile. *Drawing Interior Architecture: A Handbook of Techniques*. New York: Whitney Library of Design, 1983.

Gebhard, David, and Deborah Nevins. *200 Years of American Architectural Drawing*. New York: Whitney Library of Design, 1977.

Guptill, Arthur L., ed. by Susan E. Meyer. *Rendering in Pen and Ink*. New York: Watson-Guptill Publications, 1976.

————. *Rendering in Pencil*. New York: Watson-Guptill Publications, 1977.

Hogarth, Paul. *Drawing Architecture: A Creative Approach*. New York: Watson-Guptill Publications, 1979.

Leich, Jean Ferriss. *Architectural Visions: The Drawings of Hugh Ferriss*. New York: Whitney Library of Design, 1980.

Petrie, Ferdinand. *Drawing Landscapes in Pencil*. New York: Watson-Guptill Publications, 1979.

Pile, John (ed.). *Drawings of Architectual Interiors*. New York: Whitney Library of Design, 1979.

Probyn, Peter (ed.). *The Complete Drawing Book*. New York: Watson-Guptill Publications, 1970. Chapter entitled "Buildings" by Richard Downer.

ADDITIONAL READING

Atkin, William Wilson. *Architectural Presentation Techniques*. New York: Van Nostrand Reinhold Company, 1976.

Doblin, Jay. *Perspective: A New System for Designers*. New York: Whitney Library of Design, 1973.

Gurney, James, and Thomas Kinkade. *The Artist's Guide to Sketching: A Handbook for Drawing On-the-Spot*. New York: Watson-Guptill Publications, 1982.

Hogarth, Paul. *Creative Pencil Drawing*. New York: Watson-Guptill Publications, 1981.

Kemnitzer, Ronald. *Rendering with Markers*. New York: Watson-Guptill Publications, 1983.

Leach, Sid DelMar. *Techniques of Interior Design Rendering and Presentation*. New York: Architectural Record Books, 1977.

Oles, Paul Stevenson. *Architectural Illustration: The Value Delineation Process*. New York: Van Nostrand Reinhold Company, 1978.

Pile, John (ed.). *Drawings of Architectural Interiors*. New York: Whitney Library of Design, 1979.

Pitz, Henry C. *Charcoal Drawing*. New York: Watson-Guptill Publications, 1981.

————. *How to Draw Trees*. New York: Watson-Guptill Publications, 1980.

————. *Ink Drawing Techniques*. New York: Watson-Guptill Publications, 1957.

Ratensky, Alexander. *Drawing and Modelmaking: A Guide for Students of Architecture and Design*. New York: Whitney Library of Design, 1983.

Welling, Richard. *The Technique of Drawing Buildings*. New York: Watson-Guptill Publications, 1971.

INDEX

Numbers in italics indicate illustrations.

Edited by Susan Davis
Designed by Jay Anning
Layout by Areta Buk
Set in 10 point Caledonia